BURLINGAME
City of Trees

BURLINGAME
City of Trees

MICHAEL SVANEVIK • SHIRLEY BURGETT

Boutique & Villager
Custom & Limited Editions
San Francisco

Second Printing

Printed in Hong Kong

Designed by Morris Jackson

ISBN: 1-881529-27-4

Library of Congress Number: 97-69217

Published by
Boutique & Villager and
Custom & Limited Editions
San Francisco, California

Photographs not otherwise credited are from the authors' collection

Foreword

Burlingame always has been more than just another suburb built along the railroad tracks south of San Francisco. It is a town that has traditionally been known for its aristocratic tone.

Even the name has flair. It was named for Anson Burlingame, a 19th-century American politician and diplomat. In 1866, on a brief visit to San Francisco, he purchased land on the Peninsula before continuing his travels. Burlingame never returned. In 1870, while in Russia, he became ill and subsequently died.

There was never a Burlingame estate or house. Only his name remained. In 1893, founding members of a newly established country club took Burlingame as its name. The town soon followed.

Largely protected by hills from the strong winds and heavy fogs that often swept in from the Pacific, town pioneers nestled their community carefully between the hills and the quiet waters of San Francisco Bay. Boosters liked to advertise the town as "San Francisco's Sunshine Suburb."

The ample numbers of Indian relics and even the fossilized remains of prehistoric elephants and horses dating from the Pleistocene era, which over the years have been uncovered by builders, provided ongoing testimony to the long-term desirability of the area. Ohlone Indian shell mounds, some of them six feet in height, covered numerous half-acre expanses.

BURLINGAME
City of Trees

Anson Burlingame

Scotsman William Corbitt, a wealthy coffee merchant who acquired 440 acres of Burlingame during the early 1870s, probably was the area's first full-time resident. Corbitt discovered that the Peninsula climate was perhaps the most ideal in the world for the breeding of fine horses.

On land where Burlingame High School would later rise, Corbitt built a model breeding farm, transforming it into an equine paradise. Visitors marveled at its cleanliness as well as the meticulously built paddocks, barns and stables. Workers sprinkled and rolled his racing oval daily.

Before his death in 1898, Corbitt had achieved a worldwide reputation and shared the honor with the late Senator Leland Stanford of having bred the greatest number of champion trotters in America.

A town did not really begin to develop until the Burlingame Country Club was established in 1893. With the opening of a depot in 1894, trains regularly stopped there. A decade later, completion of an electric trolley line from San Francisco to San Mateo provided a major impetus to town growth. Nevertheless, as late as 1906 when the great California earthquake fractured San Francisco, Burlingame's population still hovered around several hundred. Of the steady stream of refugees escaping the burning city, many found sanctuary in Burlingame.

This was no accident. For Burlingame development, the earthquake was to prove fortuitous. As early as 1895, pioneer landowner William Henry Howard, whose property extended south of Burlingame Avenue, had surveyor Davenport Bromfield at work laying out streets and creating homesites.

By the turn of the 20th century, Bromfield had also surveyed much of the Corbitt tract north of Burlingame Avenue and had been retained by Ansel Mills Easton to lay out a new town along the trolley line. The town of Easton developed around a thoroughfare named Buri Buri (a name derived from an early Mexican *rancho*). Easton became part of Burlingame in 1910.

The enormous economic potential of the budding town wasn't lost on wealthy aristocratic residents, "hill people," as they were known, who, since the early 1890s, had been erecting lavish mansions with palatial gardens around the country club west of County Road. Not until 1910 did this group separate to form the town of Hillsborough.

Dean of that millionaire hill society was much respected Henry T. Scott. He was president of San Francisco's powerful Union Iron Works, the first company in the West to receive contracts to build United States ships of war.

In 1903, Scott, with his associates William H. Crocker, Francis Carolan, William S. Tevis, Joseph Grant and George Pope, acquired a portion of the former William Corbitt property where they proceeded to lay out housing plots and announced plans to construct 40 homes.

Thus, in 1906, following the earthquake, no town was better prepared nor more enthusiastic about receiving refugees than Burlingame.

From a picturesque tiny hamlet, Burlingame rapidly developed into an ideal suburban city. It became an incorporated town in May 1908.

Because of its closeness to San Francisco, Burlingame was thought of as a commuters'

Commuters catch the train at Burlingame depot, circa 1915

paradise. By 1916 when population had expanded to 4,209, the Chamber of Commerce, a group that was informally organized in 1913, proudly noted that more daily commuters boarded trains, streetcars and buses in Burlingame than in any other city of the Peninsula.

Town boosters boasted about cozy modern bungalows tastefully intermixed with stately beautiful mansions reminiscent of an Old World culture. Visitors commented on the unique marriage of carefully landscaped gardens designed to bloom the year round and the preservation of the natural artistic simplicity of the hills, fields and trees. Town trustees looked askance on homeowners who didn't keep their property quite tidy enough. Shortly after incorporation, City Hall warned property owners to keep weeds under control.

Homeowners had until the end of April each year to pull weeds. Thereafter, town Marshal George E. Jones announced that city workers would do the weeding and residents charged. Liens were placed against properties of those who neglected to pay.

But from the outset, Burlingame was more than a bedroom community. Private businesses boomed. By the mid-1920s, the town had two excellent banks and more than a dozen automobile agencies. Town fathers proudly laid claim to having the Peninsula's first "auto row." There were 35 real estate, lending agencies and insurance firms. Workers engaged in a myriad of building projects. In June 1924, 17 stores were under construction simultaneously and approval had been reached for 11 more buildings to start almost immediately.

Residents cherished Burlingame's woodsy ambience. When William Corbitt began building

*Cupola from atop town's
1914 City Hall*

his stock farm in the 1870s, the region comprised an uninteresting, windswept prairie. Under the watchful gaze of wealthy landowners the ilk of Ralston, Mills, Sharon, Howard, Corbitt and Easton, trees of many varieties were planted. Within a few years, winds were harnessed and dramatic changes took place in the appearance of the terrain. Burlingame had begun to assume a distinctive personality.

Town trustees and residents alike recognized the value of the foliage. In 1910, while other Peninsula communities were beginning to regard trees as attractive nuisances and ridding their streets of them, in Burlingame, whenever cutting could possibly be avoided, trustees denied permission to even trim street trees.

Tree-lined boulevards became a town characteristic. During the early years, Burlingame Avenue, Broadway and even the railroad tracks were lined with trees. Perhaps most famed were the great trees along County Road where Scots landscape gardener John McLaren had interspersed elms with fast-growing eucalyptus.

Burlingame residents came to revere these Australian gums. They rose in righteous wrath at the merest hint that their trees might be molested. In 1913, when a proposal was made to cut trees along County Road, the Burlingame mayor promised that anyone caught doing so would be arrested.

By the 1990s, most townsfolk recognized that the fast-growing trees were responsible for breaking sidewalks, cracking pavement and creating hazards to homes and people by randomly dropping branches and bark. Nevertheless, citizens again banded together to prevent removal. The towering eucalyptus had unquestionably come to be regarded as the "soul of the city."

Readers of this book may well encounter confusion about street names. Burlingame street names have changed over the years. Once upon a time El Camino Real was simply known as County Road; later it was referred to as the State Highway.

One main thoroughfare, San Mateo Drive, was *officially* changed in the mid-1920s to California Drive. And although Burlingame Avenue has always been such officially, previously it was also known as Corbitt Lane, Donnelly Lane and MacMonagle Lane. (Dr. B. MacMonagle was a son-in-law of William Corbitt.) By the early years of the 20th century, it was most commonly referred to simply as "the Avenue."

Main Street ran north of Burlingame Avenue. South of Burlingame Avenue it was called Middlefield Road. In January 1925, to avoid confusion, Sam Merk, editor of the *Burlingame Advance*, asked town trustees to change both names to Center Street. That name was rejected. Instead, out of respect for early Burlingame booster and realtor Frederick D. Lorton, they chose to call it Lorton Avenue.

Meanwhile, in North Burlingame, the avenue leading to Ansel M. Easton's *Black Hawk Ranch* had been called Buri Buri, a proud name chosen because it had once identified the Mexican *rancho* owned by José Antonio Sánchez.

Entry to Burlingame from the State Highway during the 1920s

But as Easton developed, residents felt increasingly uncomfortable with Buri Buri because of the sound similarity with "beriberi," a disease and nerve disorder. Thus, in November 1915, the name was changed to Broadway. (Originally, Buri Buri had been Lamphier Lane, so named for Charles Lamphier, caretaker of the Easton racetrack.)

During the 1930s, Mayor Allan Hunt, collector of Burlingame oddities, became fascinated with the realization that this was a town of drives, roads, lanes and avenues, but there were no streets in Burlingame.

Town residents always have revered Burlingame history. Following the Loma Prieta earthquake of 1989, they elected, at considerable extra expense, to reproduce the town's historic fire station rather than adopt a new and modern design.

Additionally, in 1992, the old fire bell, once used to summon volunteer firemen, was mounted in front of the rebuilt firehouse on California Drive. After the destruction of the 1914 City Hall, its delicate cupola was transformed into a monument on an island in a parking lot where the building once stood on Park Road south of Burlingame Avenue.

Meanwhile, the town's First Congregational Church, a sturdy shingled building erected in 1907, later housed the public library after the church disbanded in 1912. This structure subsequently was moved and used as the American Legion Hall. By the last years of the century, meetings of the local Lions Club convened there.

In 1985, when the 19th-century railroad depot was literally disintegrating, citizens recognized

its historic value and the structure was painstakingly restored.

Perhaps appropriately, the city, in 1986, turned over the old Carriage House on the Moses Gunst estate in Washington Park for use as the archive of the Burlingame Historical Society. The organization was allowed to lease the building for $2 a year.

During the 1990s, when it was announced that the 1931 library would be wrecked to make way for a modern state-of-the-art facility, many citizens expressed sadness that the town would be losing the old building whose distinctive facade had come to characterize Burlingame's center of reading and learning. After negotiations, a compromise was reached.

In spring 1996, when the old building came down, contractors carefully preserved its unique front, designed by esteemed Burlingame architect Ernest L. Norberg.

Despite extra expense, not only the facade but the children's and the reference rooms, considered to have been the heart of the old building, were maintained.

The new structure rose and, at the appropriate moment, was masterfully appended to the historic 60-year old sections.

Contractors were warned to protect six aged street trees on Primrose and Bellevue. A single large deodar pine, in front of the structure, was painstakingly fenced to prevent possible damage. To the chagrin of the Library Board, one tree, whose roots threatened the building, had to be removed. All others were saved.

Perhaps few episodes better capture the spirit of Burlingame.

BURLINGAME
City of Trees

*The San Francisco &
San José Railroad,
completed along the Peninsula
in 1864, was photographed
near Burlingame 20 years
later. The photographer
captured the bleakness
of the terrain.*

Pill Box Station

Oak Grove or *Pill Box Station*, a flag stop dating from the mid-1860s, was located north of the present depot. It had been erected by Joseph H. Redington, who was often referred to as the area's first commuter. When he wanted to board a train, he simply flagged one down.

The station was little more than a dinky shed. It was almost completely isolated; no other structures were nearby. It stood in the shade of towering eucalyptus trees that kept it cool during summer and dark throughout most of the day.

Tramps who walked the railroad line and stopped at Oak Grove to rest frequently carved their initials on the walls.

After establishment of the Burlingame Country Club, that organization's members found tiny Oak Grove Station inadequate as a depot. They requested that Southern Pacific construct a new one. Initially, the railroad declined to become involved.

William Ralston

William Sharon

Joseph Henry Poett, M.D.

Anson Burlingame

Joseph Henry Poett, M.D.

Dominant among Burlingame pioneers was Dr. Joseph Henry Poett, father of Agnes Poett Howard. Upon the death of her husband, William Davis Merry Howard (1856), Dr. Poett inherited a third of the Howard estate. This included parts of Burlingame (south of Burlingame Avenue) and most of what later separated to become Hillsborough.

Poett, in May 1866, sold 1,043 acres to diplomat Anson Burlingame during a brief visit by the latter to California. The price was $54,757. Burlingame died (February 23, 1870) in St. Petersburg, Russia, without returning.

The land passed to San Francisco banker William C. Ralston. He had the hills planted in trees. By 1874, he talked of laying out a town with large villa lots, broad avenues and shade trees. He planned to call the community *Ralstonville*. Ralston died in August 1875. Except for tree planting (west of County Road) none of his plan had been acted upon.

The land passed to his partner William Sharon. Thereon, Sharon built the Palace Hotel Dairy to produce milk, cream and butter for the huge San Francisco caravansary.

Sharon died in 1886. Francis G. Newlands, a son-in-law and executor of his estate, conceived the plan for a millionaire colony to rise around a country club.

The Easton home was one of the show places of North Burlingame.

MARK STILL

Easton family

Native New Yorker Ansel (commonly called Tony) Ives Easton, an early arrival to California during the Gold Rush, married Adeline Mills, sister of Darius Ogden Mills (1857). Along with Mills, Easton was one of the earliest landowners in what became North Burlingame. He built *Black Hawk Ranch*, originally called by Easton "Home Farm," and was a breeder of thoroughbred horses.

In association with other breeders, Easton laid out a race track known as Shell Mound Park because the track was paved with crushed shells gathered from nearby Indian mounds. It was located in the area of later Broadway and Rollins Road.

Easton's home, erected in 1858 (near Jackling and Armsby drives) as a present to his wife, was constructed of adobe. It crumbled in the earthquake of October 1868, several months after the builder's death.

His widow built a luxurious 40-room mansion on the old home site, set amid 80 acres improved like a city park. Easton's son, Ansel Mills Easton, sold parts of the property to home seekers after the earthquake of 1906. The house sold in 1917 for a then staggering $400,000.

Ansel I. Easton's daughter, Jennie, married Charles Frederick Crocker, eldest son of the transcontinental railroad builder.

SAN MATEO COUNTY HISTORICAL MUSEUM

A woman, believed to be Adeline Mills Easton, photographed on a Black Hawk thoroughbred. The elegant image was snapped in a studio.

Anson Burlingame

Though the town was named for him, Anson Burlingame never lived there. In fact, his visit was exceedingly brief.

A New England politician, Burlingame was nominated in 1861 by Abraham Lincoln to serve as the first U.S. Minister to the Court of Peking. He emerged as leader of the diplomatic community while encouraging the Chinese to establish ties with the West.

In 1866, en route to Washington, Burlingame visited the Peninsula where he was entertained at Belmont by William C. Ralston. Thereafter, before returning to his post, he purchased from Dr. Joseph H. Poett 1,100 acres in what became Burlingame.

Apparently Burlingame hoped to return, build a home and, with Ralston, coordinate trade between the United States and China. But in 1867, at the behest of Chinese officials, he resigned his American position and was employed to lead the first Chinese embassy to the West to establish diplomatic ties with the United States and the powers of Europe.

His success was China's first diplomatic triumph. A trade treaty was signed in Washington in July 1868. Subsequent treaties were concluded with Britain, France, Prussia, Sweden, Norway, Denmark and Russia.

Burlingame died of pneumonia in Russia in 1870. His casket, draped with the flag of China, was returned to Boston for burial.

Anson Burlingame was Lincoln's choice to be the American Minister to Peking.

Burlingame, serving as China's Ambassador to the World, sat (second from right) for a photograph with the Chinese Imperial Embassy in San Francisco (1868). The standing Caucasian was Sir J. McLeavy of Great Britain, First Secretary to the mission. Seated to the left is Frenchman M. Deschamps, the Second Secretary. Burlingame is flanked on the left by Chikang, a Manchu prince and on the right by Sun Chai-ku, Imperial Commissioner. The standing mandarins have never been identified.

Burlingame was buried at Mount Auburn Cemetery in Cambridge, Massachusetts.

This single photograph exists of Avitor's *flight at Shell Park*.

Scientific American *(December 4, 1869) included a drawing and story on the flight of* Avitor.

Avitor: *Amazing aerial device demonstrated*

No journalist had been invited. William H. Seward, former American Secretary of State, was the single notable to observe this private test flight staged by the Aerial Steam Navigation Company of San Francisco, July 2, 1869.

The porpoise-shaped, balloon-like device, 30 feet in length, was designed by San Francisco inventor Frederick Marriott and officially known as the *Avitor Hermes Jr.*

Wings, covered with cloth located back of the center of the carriage, were attached to the frame by wires. Two steam-driven, four-foot propellers were placed in the framework of the wings. Propellers rotated at 100 revolutions per minute, adequately fast to keep *Avitor* aloft and moving at a fair rate of speed. When not filled with gas, the craft weighed 84 pounds.

The almost-secret test was made at Shell Park on a track owned by the Ansel I. Easton family in North Burlingame.

Scientific American (July 1869) reported: "With the first turn of the propellers she rose [75 feet] slowly into the air, gradually increasing speed until the rate of five miles an hour was attained."

The European press quickly grasped the meaning of *Avitor's* success. Engineers were convinced that a larger machine, capable of carrying passengers, could be constructed.

Frederick Marriott

5

The 42-room Mills house was erected in 1870.

MILLBRAE HISTORICAL SOCIETY

Darius Ogden Mills

SAN FRANCISCO PUBLIC LIBRARY

Mills called his home Happy House

Until his death in 1910, banker D.O. Mills, since the 1880s a resident of New York, wintered at his Peninsula estate.

During the 1860s, Mills had paid $15 an acre for 1,500 acres of what had been part of the Mexican *rancho* owned by José Antonio Sánchez. In 1870, Mills built a three-story structure patterned on a French mansard-roofed chateau. The 42-room mansion of Second Empire architectural styling became a county showplace.

One bedroom was always known as the General Grant Suite, commemorating a visit, in 1879, by the former president. In fact, however, Grant never slept in the house.

After the death of Mills, his children and grandchildren continued to visit. During World War II, the home served as a convalescent center for the U.S. Merchant Marine.

The estate sold to developers in 1953. Peninsulans hoped to see the house preserved. There was talk of turning it into a private school or church. In August 1953, 4,000 were there to watch society matrons take part in a fashion show for the Crippled Children's Society. Workers began house demolition in 1954. It was engulfed by flames June 23.

Located in unincorporated San Mateo County, the house had long been claimed by both Millbrae and North Burlingame. While the gardens surrounding it extended into Burlingame, the house was in Millbrae.

Livery men pose on the porch of the William Corbitt stables. The building was one constructed by John Donnelly.

Corbitt Stock Farm

Stock breeder William Corbitt was believed to have been the first to settle in what became the town of Burlingame. His 440 acres, acquired during the 1870s, comprised all the land north of Burlingame Avenue and extended from County Road to the bay. Corbitt built a model stock farm.

Corbitt's barns and stables, approximately where the high school was erected during the 1920s, were built by Burlingame carpenter John Donnelly. In payment for services, Donnelly received five acres of Corbitt land west of San Mateo Drive.

His best stock was shipped each year to New York for the horse show and usually took top prizes. Along with Leland Stanford, Corbitt achieved a worldwide reputation. The two shared the honor of breeding the greatest number of champion trotters in America.

In 1882, Corbitt purchased Guy Wilkes. This great horse proved the best investment in horseflesh he ever made. In five years on the turf, the progeny of Guy Wilkes won races for the sum of $119,156. It was asserted that Corbitt realized over $450,000 from the sale of horses from his farm.

Before his death in 1898, Corbitt sold his property to Francis J. Carolan, and thereafter it was known as *Crossways Farm*.

Regal Wilkes was son of Corbitt's famed champion Guy Wilkes. He was positioned for a photograph on the Corbitt track.

Trees and town beautification

In 1854, California's Episcopal Bishop William I. Kip described the Peninsula landscape as a "vast prairie" void of fences and houses. "Here and there we see herds of wild cattle, easily distinguished from the domestic by...large branching horns, or groups of wild horses grazing about...then a herdsman wrapped in his *serape*, would pass, with huge spurs jingling like bells."

Indeed, "a treeless waste." Almost every day, during autumn, winter and spring, winds swept along the corridor between San Mateo and Millbrae making it, some felt, unfit for habitation.

During the early 1870s, banker William C. Ralston and local landowners D.O. Mills and George Howard became determined to plant trees and, in the process, improve the climate.

Planting began in 1874 under the supervision of John Donnelly. Plans called for alternating red gum, blue gum, acacia, pepper, elms, pines and cypress. Earliest planting was accomplished primarily west of County Road in what became Hillsborough.

Donnelly fenced many trees to provide protection from the herds of cattle frequently driven up the Peninsula.

A proposed tree removal plan in 1916 was strenuously opposed because it would leave Burlingame at the peril of savage winds.

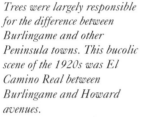

Trees were largely responsible for the difference between Burlingame and other Peninsula towns. This bucolic scene of the 1920s was El Camino Real between Burlingame and Howard avenues.

BURLINGAME PUBLIC LIBRARY

Built at what became Burlingame Avenue and Primrose Road, the Donnelly home was one of the first in the area.

John Donnelly

Minnesota-born John Donnelly came to California in 1859. He taught himself carpentry from books. He was employed by stock breeder William Corbitt and constructed all of the Corbitt barns and stables.

Donnelly purchased five acres north of Burlingame Avenue between Primrose and Park roads. Thereon, in 1876 he built what was probably the first family home in Burlingame.

The distinctive structure, ultimately wrecked to make way for a parking lot in 1964, was a square, solid, two-story, wood frame house with shuttered windows. Highlighting it were a windmill and a water tower. Surrounded by a picket fence, the house was set in the middle of the acreage. Along with his close friend, Scots landscaper John McLaren, who later became superintendent of San Francisco's Golden Gate Park, Donnelly created a garden-like effect by setting out more than 1,000 fruit trees and shrubs.

Donnelly built his home when Burlingame Avenue was still private property and blocked by two large gates, one on County Road and the other near the bay marsh. Both gates bore signs warning people to "keep out."

In 1915, as businesses began to encroach on Burlingame Avenue, Donnelly's house was moved a block north to what became Donnelly Avenue.

BURLINGAME HISTORICAL SOCIETY

John Donnelly, one of the town's earliest residents, was photographed in 1858 before leaving Minnesota for California.

William Henry Howard

William Henry Howard (b. 1850), son of Gold Rush pioneer William Davis Merry Howard, was raised by his mother, Agnes Poett Howard, and a stepfather. Following the death of her first husband in 1856, Agnes married George Howard (her former brother-in-law).

William Henry was sent abroad for schooling, spending many years away from the Peninsula.

Howard later inherited property south of Burlingame Avenue, then a jackrabbit-and coyote-infested wheat field. He established a dairy while cultivating hay and raising a herd of blooded shorthorn cattle.

By the late 1880s, he was devising plans to subdivide. In 1895, surveyor Davenport Bromfield was laying out avenues adjoining the depot on both sides of the tracks.

In Howard's development, streets were laid out in blocks. Bromfield also subdivided William Corbitt's property. There, streets were curved in an effort to avoid the necessity of building bridges to cross the creeks.

Howard died in 1901.

In 1898, this was the scene on east Burlingame Avenue looking west from the entrance to the Carolan Polo Field.

BURLINGAME PUBLIC LIBRARY

ST. MATTHEW'S EPISCOPAL CHURCH

William H. Howard (left) was photographed as a young man, during the 1860s, on the porch of El Cerrito, the family home in San Mateo.

Burlingame Country Club

In 1886, upon the death of William Sharon who owned most of the hill property, then still Burlingame (later Hillsborough), control of the land passed to his son-in-law, Francis Newlands.

Newlands began to develop "Burlingame Park." Sixteen acres of a planned 750-acre suburb were laid out. San Francisco Golden Gate Park Superintendent John McLaren undertook the landscaping. An architect designed luxurious English-style cottages.

Buyers were promised an exclusive colony of summer homes with tree-lined roads, lawn tennis courts, croquet grounds, polo fields, spouting fountains and other essential embellishments.

Newlands pledged that the jewel of Burlingame Park was to be a country club. Excited by its possibilities, wealthy San Franciscans established the Burlingame Club, as first known, in September 1893. The clubhouse, first of five, was on County Road at Bellevue. This organization gradually developed into one of the West's most prestigious social institutions.

It has always been called the Burlingame Country Club. Nevertheless, since 1910, its location has been in incorporated Hillsborough.

The town, dating from the 1890s, has often jokingly been referred to as "Blingum." This was a dig at the Anglophile mannerisms of the country club set.

Architect George H. Howard Jr. designed this elegant structure for the Burlingame Club in 1899. It burned in 1910.

This scene, the back patio of the Country Club, 1912-1955, came to symbolize the leisurely lifestyle of the "hill people."

11

Burlingame's Southern Pacific depot became the town's most enduring advertisement.

George H. Howard Jr.

Prettiest station on the Southern Pacific line

Faced with the reality that Southern Pacific would not build a prestigious station to mollify the Burlingame Country Club, its members came up with most of the $8,000 necessary for construction.

In 1894, a structure was designed by architects George H. Howard Jr. and Joachim B. Mathisen. They capitalized on a nostalgia for California's mission heritage, building the world's first Mission Revival depot.

The tile roof was a unique feature. Tiles were acquired from the decaying Mission San Antonio de Padua at Jolon. The Spanish mission, third in the Golden Chain, had been erected in 1771. Other tiles came from ruins of the San Mateo Mission Hospice, the Peninsula's original structure dating from the 1790s. Thus while the depot dated from 1894, its roof was between 100 and 120 years older.

No other Burlingame building generated so much civic pride. It drew the attention of thousands of commuters. The depot became the community's most enduring advertisement.

It became a California Historical Landmark in 1971 and was added to the National Register of Historic Places in 1978. National recognition was given on the basis of its design alone.

Sand pirates

The sandy beach and sheltered swimming cove at Coyote Point, shared as a recreational facility by San Mateo and Burlingame, was one of the area's most celebrated attractions. But, by 1894, it was in serious danger. A threat was posed by thieving schooner captains intent on making off with the beach, literally. "If thefts continue, our beach will be ruined for bathing purposes," declared angry officials.

For years, "sand pirates" visited Coyote Point solely to steal sand, carrying away 50 to 100 tons per shipload. In 1894 alone, Peter Rogers, in charge of the bath house, prevented 15 schooner captains from taking the valuable substance aboard.

Pirates, intent on gathering the sand for sale in San Francisco to artificial stone manufacturers, had already rendered large portions of Coyote Point beach unusable. Entire sections were characterized by rock and mud.

Modesty and community standards dictated that beach wear wasn't too brief.

Coyote Point beach attracted the children of Burlingame.

Davenport Bromfield

Davenport Bromfield, perhaps Burlingame's most significant pioneer, died in 1954. Almost singlehandedly he had shaped the town—literally.

During the 1890s, he was hired by landowner William H. Howard to lay out streets south of Burlingame Avenue. After 1900, he subdivided portions of William Corbitt's horse breeding farm. In 1905, Ansel M. Easton retained him to plat Easton. Five years later he surveyed for the new town site of Hillsborough. Bromfield also did surveys for the Burlingame and Hillsborough sewer systems.

Born in Australia (1862), Bromfield studied surveying at the University of Melbourne. In his early twenties, he fled the country with Mary Ware, the woman he loved. Already married and the mother of three, this resident of the harsh Outback (with a baby daughter), abandoned her family, opting for life in America with the handsome surveyor, 12 years her junior.

They arrived in San Francisco in 1883. Pillars of local society, they became parents of four.

Members of the Bromfield family were photographed at their Tilton Avenue (San Mateo) home in 1889. Beatrice, daughter of Mary Bromfield and her legal husband, is seated next to her mother. The surveyor is at right. Between are two sons, D. Gordon and John.

SAN MATEO COUNTY HISTORICAL MUSEUM

BURLINGAME HISTORICAL SOCIETY

Residents Frank Wilkinson, Wilkie J. Dessin and Harry Dessin went goose hunting on the Burlingame marsh in 1918.

So many ducks inhabited the marsh that the sky often seemed to be darkened by them.

Marsh was duck haven

During the late 19th and early 20th centuries, the marsh along the county's Bay side was part of the Pacific Flyway, a layover spot for migrating ducks and geese heading south from breeding grounds in Canada.

In fall, they swept in by the thousands. The assortment couldn't be equaled anywhere else in California.

October to January were the biggest duck months. In calm weather, they were seen in flocks floating on the water or sleeping on mud banks, heads tucked beneath their wings. Mornings and evenings the sky came alive with birds.

Peninsula lads received shotguns before long pants. Weekends, Southern Pacific added a "hunters' car" to Peninsula-bound trains. It was outfitted with gunracks and game hooks. Hunters could be accompanied by faithful retrievers.

Sportsmen did little harm to the flocks. But "market hunters," who shot game for sale, did horrendous damage. Utilizing unsportsmanly techniques, such as shotgun-like cannons, they often killed up to 100 birds with as few as four or six shots.

By 1900, the county's duck population had declined by half. A season was established in 1891. The first limit, imposed in 1901, restricted a hunter to 50 birds per day.

Frank Thrall (left) and Rod McLellan, snapped at play near the McLellan home on Bayswater Avenue in 1919. Thrall became a Burlingame businessman; McLellan excelled in floral enterprises.

BURLINGAME HISTORICAL SOCIETY

McLellan's Nursery

BURLINGAME HISTORICAL SOCIETY

E.W. McLellan's nursery, largest glass house complex west of the Mississippi.

Town population was well below 200 in 1895 when Edgar Wakefield McLellan purchased land bounded by Howard and Burlingame avenues, east of California Drive.

Of almost 80 nurseries on the Peninsula, McLellan's became the most productive. Flowers grew in open fields and 13 glass houses. It was the largest growing complex west of Chicago.

By 1902, 200,000 roses were harvested a month and the hothouses produced 4,000 dozen carnations. Monthly yields included 5,000 dozen lilies of the valley, 5,000 ferns and 18,000 chrysanthemums. In spring, McLellan's produced 10,000 Easter lilies.

McLellan was the first to ship chrysanthemums beyond San Francisco successfully by using refrigerated rail cars. His flowers sold all over the West and occasionally as far away as New York.

While the fragrance of McLellan flowers spread across the nation, manure and other odors associated with horticulture became too much for the delicate people of Burlingame. After E.W. McLellan's retirement in 1930, the nursery was dismantled and moved to unincorporated Colma, near South San Francisco.

In 1900, George W. Gates built a family home near the depot on the north side of Burlingame Avenue.

George W. Gates family

Of Burlingame pioneers, none stands taller than George W. Gates, who stepped off a train at the new depot with his bride of three days, in June 1895.

The San Francisco-born Gates, an employee of Southern Pacific, had been hired as Burlingame's third station master. In addition he became the telegraph operator, Wells Fargo agent and town postmaster. He and his wife lived in one end of the station "because there was no other place for us." His first son, George Clifton Gates, was born in the depot.

The family constructed a shingled house on Burlingame Avenue in 1900. Sixteen years later, as businesses encroached, the house was placed on rollers and moved north to Donnelly Avenue.

On the original site, Gates supervised construction of the Garden Theatre. In an area of the lobby, his son, Robert W. Gates, opened Gentleman's Fine Neckwear, a tie shop, in 1921. This ultimately developed into an exclusive clothing store for men and women. In 1942, the store moved two blocks west on Burlingame Avenue, where it remained a landmark until closing in 1991.

Jessie Murphy (left) and George Clifton Gates posed in front of the a palm tree at the railroad depot in 1901. Gates was born in the depot.

Fast growing eucalyptus trees gave early residents the impression that the trees had always been there.

Burlingame Avenue at the turn of the century

During the 19th century, Burlingame Avenue was the dividing line between Corbitt property to the north and land owned by William Henry Howard to the south.

Until shortly after 1900, the street was lined with rows of densely planted eucalyptus trees, blue gums, the toughest of the eucalyptus family. As a boy, Davenport G. Bromfield recalled riding his horse along the Avenue when there were perhaps two buildings west of the tracks, the most noticeable having been the home of builder John Donnelly.

Development of what became Burlingame's main street required the cutting down and rooting out of these trees.

During the earliest years of the town, Burlingame Avenue was frequently, though never officially, known as Corbitt's Lane and later Donnelly Lane.

Burlingame was bleak during the first years of the century. The photograph was taken on the George W. Gates property near Burlingame Avenue.

Frank Carolan's elegant polo pavilion was a point of meeting for many of America's most fashionable families. Musicians played beneath the striped awning atop the structure.

A polo match at Crossways Farm was always an occasion to don one's finest costume.

Crossways Farm

Handsome Francis Carolan married heiress Harriet Pullman, daughter of the Chicago sleeping car magnate, in 1892. Five years later they built spectacular *Crossways*, a 30-room Burlingame home at the junction of Willow and Sharon avenues. There Carolan maintained one of the finest private stables in Western America.

In 1901, Carolan purchased a 172-acre portion of William Corbitt Horse Ranch in east Burlingame extending from the railroad tracks to the Bay, and called it *Crossways Farm*.

At one time Carolan maintained 94 trotters and polo ponies. To the existing racetrack, Carolan added a polo field that, for years, was used by country club teams.

He built a polo pavilion, soon a meeting place for America's social elite, including the Vanderbilts, Harrimans and Rockefellers. Carolan greeted guests in white knickerbockers and powder-blue riding coat, his stable's colors.

Coaching parties were perhaps the smart set's most exhilarating pastime. Few were more adept at handling the great carriages than Carolan himself. Carolan owned 25 carriages; none cost him less than $1,000.

Crossways Farm was the center of Burlingame's horsey society. This photo was taken in 1901, the year Carolan acquired the property from the Corbitt estate.

BURLINGAME PUBLIC LIBRARY

*Grading for the interurban
electric railway began near
Burlingame about 1900.*

The interurban trolley

TOM GRAY

*Frequent trolleys transformed
Burlingame into San
Francisco's favorite suburb.*

New Year's Day, 1903. United Railroads of San Francisco had done the deed and the big, drafty interurban trolleys came rumbling through town. By the day's end, 900 excited non-residents had seen Burlingame. An electric trolley had been the dream of developers since the early 1890s. Only a decade later did the line receive a numerical designation and become known variously as "the 40 Car," "Car No. 40" or "Car 40."

The line began at Fifth and Market streets in San Francisco, ran along Mission to Daly City, past the cemeteries, and then down the Peninsula running parallel to the railroad tracks from San Bruno to San Mateo. The line ended in a loop adjacent to the San Mateo train depot between Second and Third avenues.

Initially, trolleys operated hourly. When the line was in full operation, streetcars moved on a 20-minute headway between 6 a.m. and 1 a.m.

The president's arrival in Burlingame was a long-awaited event. Seated next to Roosevelt is Henry T. Scott.

Theodore Roosevelt, a consummate politician, took time to greet children on the steps of the Burlingame Country Club.

Burlingame rolls out the red carpet

In the town's early history, no single day was more anticipated than May 14, 1903, when President Theodore Roosevelt arrived to lunch with members of the Burlingame Country Club.

The depot was crowded with admirers. Perhaps there never had been a more impressive display of elegant carriages. Francis Carolan, country club president, had acquired a new Victoria expressly for the purposes of carrying the popular president to lunch. Roosevelt shared the carriage with Henry T. Scott, powerful San Francisco industrialist, ship builder, land developer and founding father of Hillsborough.

In 1948, residents again rolled out the red carpet for a brief stop by campaigning President Harry S. Truman who addressed a crowd at the depot from the observation car of the *Presidential Special*.

President Harry S. Truman stopped long enough in Burlingame for him to address crowds at the depot in 1948.

TOM GRAY

Extra trolleys were put into service during school commute hours or when there were racing events at Tanforan in San Bruno.

TOM GRAY

A trolley of the Market Street Railway heading north (1942) in front of the Broadway depot.

Trolley changed Burlingame

This additional means of transportation was a major impetus to suburban growth. New interest in local properties was immediately evident as San Francisco real estate offices, for the first time, became Peninsula-minded. Surveyor Davenport Bromfield, who had previously platted land south of Burlingame Avenue, now began to subdivide one-time Corbitt property to the north of the Avenue. San Francisco industrialist Henry T. Scott and his associates acquired land and had lots laid out. Landholder Ansel M. Easton also began the town of Easton in North Burlingame. Companies were created to handle sales in new tracts. One, Lyon & Hoag, maintained offices in San Francisco and another near the Burlingame depot.

After the opening of Burlingame High School during the 1920s, streetcars brought scores of youngsters from Daly City, Lomita Park, Millbrae and other parts of North San Mateo County. The picture of extra cars lined up in front of Burlingame depot wasn't an unusual one.

TOM GRAY

Trolley tracks were laid through town in 1902. The streetcar line gave impetus to development of the business area.

Burlingame Square

During Burlingame's earliest years, land immediately around the depot, donated to the town, was in the form of a circle and was the only paved area in Burlingame. Later, the configuration changed and it became commonly known as "Burlingame Square."

Fronting the square were five wood buildings, constructed following the turn of the century. These were the drugstore (which also housed the post office), a grocery built by W.P. Archibald, Brown Brothers Blacksmith (owned by William Brown, who later became a San Mateo County Supervisor), the Husing building and the Hatch building. Hatch's was one of the first business buildings erected in town; it was a saloon and small hotel on the southwest corner of San Mateo Drive and Burlingame Avenue.

After the town's incorporation, a police bell, to summon an officer, was hung in the square. This could be rung by telephone control. Later, a system of blinking red lights was installed to prompt officers to telephone the office.

This area, seen from the depot, had once been Burlingame Square. The corner building at right was originally Burlingame Bank. Next to it along the Avenue was the Masonic Hall.

23

Newspapers of the community

Until publication was finally suspended in May 1973, the *Burlingame Advance Star* had been the newspaper of the community.

It was founded in 1905 as the *Advance* by Fritz W. Dickey, L.E. Fuller and W. H. Hanscomb. It was published weekly. In 1907, the paper was sold to F.W. Atkinson and two years thereafter to Sam D. Merk, a California journalist of note. Under Merk, the *Advance* was published semi-weekly.

A competitive newspaper, the *Burlingame Star*, an enterprise of Horace W. Amphlett, publisher of the *San Mateo Times*, began in January 1923. Merk purchased the Amphlett newspaper in 1925 and created the *Burlingame Advance Star*, the town's first daily and the second daily in San Mateo County.

Responding to the community's apparent desire for more "weekly fashion news, exotic recipes, garden tips and church news," the *Hillsborough Boutique* began publication in 1965.

The *Burlingame Villager* first appeared in 1971. These two newspapers were later combined to create the *Burlingame-Hillsborough Boutique & Villager*.

This newspaper was philosophically dedicated to reporting local news and supporting community charities and fundraisers in addition to being a billboard for local advertising. The twice weekly *Boutique & Villager* is now one of the seven newspapers of the Independent Newspaper Group published by Ted Fang.

Historically, the Burlingame-Hillsborough Boutique & Villager *was supportive of fund-raising events such as the Hillsborough Concours d'Elegance, an annual affair to generate money for the public schools. Local resident, crooner Bing Crosby, lent his name to the event in 1967 when he was snapped by a* Boutique *photographer.*

By the night of April 18, 1906, San Francisco's downtown was aflame and thousands were fleeing the city.

Earthquake of 1906

No event had a more significant impact on the growth of Burlingame than the earthquake of April 18, 1906. Hundreds of city dwellers seeking refuge from the inferno that was San Francisco sought sanctuary in Burlingame.

Before the disaster, the population of the small Peninsula hamlet had hovered around 200. In the days after it, County Road became clogged with refugees escaping the city.

Within a year, Burlingame grew to 1,000; by 1914, the population was 2,849. No Northern California town since the hectic days of the Gold Rush had expanded more rapidly.

Refugees found immediate shelter in tents, cabins and shacks. Lots sold and tents were soon replaced by comfortable homes.

Although Burlingame residents themselves had suffered in the earthquake when houses had been thrown from foundations and chimneys toppled, many former San Franciscans felt, by comparison, that the Peninsula was still a safer place to be.

Earthquake refugees camped all along the Peninsula. Many stayed permanently in Burlingame.

The never-incorporated town of Easton became part of Burlingame in 1910.

Ansel Mills Easton (left) on the veranda of the family home in 1900, discussing the development of North Burlingame with an unidentified subdivider.

Town of Easton

In 1857, Ansel Ives Easton acquired 1,500 acres south of the D.O. Mills property (later North Burlingame).

Easton died at age 49 in 1868. While his widow maintained the family estates, their son, Ansel Mills Easton, in need of cash at the turn of the century, chose to join the trend toward subdivision. Surveyor Davenport Bromfield laid out building lots. A small depot called Easton was built to accommodate land patrons.

By 1906, the laying out of lots was already complete. The earthquake merely stimulated sales.

The town was Easton. Its eucalyptus-lined main thoroughfare called Buri Buri, a name taken from the early Mexican *rancho*, was later renamed Broadway, which also became the name of the depot.

After a number of attempts to unite Burlingame and Easton, proponents triumphed in 1910 and the so-called Easton Addition became part of the city. North Burlingame had been known as Easton for approximately four years.

Home built to last

George Farrell, a bricklayer born in 1863, arrived in San Francisco from England at the age of 27. He became well-known as a contractor and builder. He was the general contractor of the California Academy of Sciences, St. Luke's Hospital and both the Crocker and Hobart buildings.

Acting as both architect and builder, in 1905, Farrell began Burlingame's first clinker brick residence. Under construction at the time of the earthquake of 1906, the house was badly damaged. Thus, Farrell incorporated techniques to assure the home's longevity on the unstable ground. Bricks were anchored by using a heavy wire interlacing. Iron girders were embedded between floors.

Fashioned in the style of an English manor house, the 1427 Chapin Avenue home was a town showplace. Characterizing the elegant structure were hand-fashioned brick trimmings and arches around the windows and cornices. Interior woodwork was carved to match the curve and design of exterior bricks. Bathroom floors were marble rescued from the original Palace Hotel in San Francisco. The floor of the front porch was imported marble, supported by round brick columns.

In 1968, the Farrell house became part of the Burlingame Garden Center, which had started business next door to the house immediately following World War II.

The George Farrell family in front of the home meticulously constructed during and after the earthquake of 1906.

From the time of its completion in 1894, the depot served Burlingame as a community center and meeting place.

BURLINGAME HISTORICAL SOCIETY

Depot seating was used not only by commuters but members of churches and civic organizations as well.

Depot was more than a ticket office

Few buildings so thoroughly captured the spirit of a community. In addition to being a ticket office, it once housed Wells Fargo Express, Western Union Telegraph, the Pacific Telephone switchboard and Burlingame's first U.S. Post Office.

The town's First Baptist Church, beginning July 15, 1906, held services in the depot's waiting room until its small shingled church was completed October 25, 1908. Sunday school classes and early meetings of the Burlingame Woman's Club were held there. Fox hunts sponsored by the Burlingame Country Club began at the station. Red-jacketed riders and baying hounds gathered in front to await the call of the hunter's horn.

The unique structure was renovated in 1985 at a cost of $300,000, portions of which were contributed by the Burlingame City Council, the citizens of the town and the state of California. In 1987, the Burlingame Chamber of Commerce set up offices in the south end of the depot.

Mr. Turrell, Mr. Miller, young Gladys Reighley and her parents, Mr. and Mrs. L.G. Reighley, were guests on the Winchester ark about 1908.

BURLINGAME HISTORICAL SOCIETY

Sarah Winchester's Ark

Neighbors whispered about the sanity of Sarah L. Winchester, a widow, who maintained a double-floored ark set upon a man-made island surrounded by a canal on the Bay marsh extending from Oak Grove to Broadway. Access to the ark, complete with bedroom, living room, kitchen and bath, was via an artistic footbridge imported from Asia.

Winchester, said to be haunted by spirits of unfortunate wretches killed throughout the West by Winchester rifles, was awaiting *the* flood.

Upon the death of her husband, William Wirt Winchester (son of the founder of Winchester Repeating Rifle Company) in 1881, the lady inherited a $20 million fortune.

Three years later, she purchased an eight-room home in Santa Clara County. This she called her "hobby house" and allegedly spent $5 million on it. (The so-called Winchester Mystery House, with more than 160 rooms, later became a major tourist attraction.)

Winchester acquired 35 Burlingame acres in 1906. A seawall was constructed to control Bay waters while canals and floodgates were planned to accommodate visitors arriving by yachts. Winchester hoped to build a country estate there but never did.

This ark wasn't unique. Such houseboats, many extremely luxurious, had been popular on the Bay as early as the 1880s as comfortable summer refuges. It burned in 1929. The lady seldom visited Burlingame.

BURLINGAME HISTORICAL SOCIETY

An ornate wood bridge connected the ark with solid land.

Dr. Archie L. Offield

Until 1907, when a doctor was needed in Burlingame, one was summoned from Redwood City. And then, it took half a day for him to arrive—by train. It mattered not what the ailment was, the cost was still $2.

Dr. Archie Leonard Offield, who arrived in March 1907, was the town's first resident physician. Born in Oregon (1877), Offield had graduated from Cooper Medical School in San Francisco in 1905. Before coming to Burlingame, he served an internship at the Southern Pacific Hospital and worked briefly at Santa Clara Hospital.

Offield made house calls in a buggy pulled by his faithful horse Bracelet, an animal once owned by William H. Crocker. In addition to private practice, Offield was appointed physician for the Peninsula Theatre (1926), medical superintendent for San Mateo Community Hospital (1927) and Burlingame police surgeon (1928). He was also a member of the San Mateo County Board of Health.

Dr. Archie Offield seen with his automobile, circa World War I.

ARCHIE OFFIELD

BURLINGAME WOMAN'S CLUB

The first clubhouse constructed by the Burlingame Woman's Club in 1912.

Burlingame Woman's Club

Until Mrs. George B. Miller came along, Burlingame lacked trees, sidewalks and paved streets. Life was uncomfortable. Residents were plagued by flies and mosquitoes, while choking on dust or wading through mud.

Flea-bitten curs, strays whose only purpose in life seemed to be to chase pampered cats, lurked the streets. In an era when abstinence was considered a virtue, alcoholic beverages were amazingly easy to acquire.

Mary Merrill Miller and other strenuous middle-class town dames decided in 1907 that things had to change. The first meeting of the Woman's Club was held at the Southern Pacific depot May 31, 1907. Civic betterment and beautification were the avowed purposes.

These ladies spearheaded a move to curtail the "vile traffic in intoxicants." Unsightly billboards were outlawed. An expert with a shotgun was deputized to rid Burlingame of the "stray dog nuisance once and for all."

The club waged war against flies, mosquitoes, free-wandering chickens, filthy cuspidors, uncovered food on counters and cigarette sales to young boys. The ladies championed house numbering, free home mail delivery, better sanitary services and improved schools.

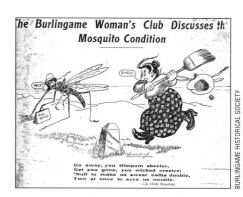

BURLINGAME HISTORICAL SOCIETY

Burlingame women launched a major crusade against mosquitoes.

Bellevue Avenue homes in 1908 indicate spacious, comfortable dwellings. Streets are still unpaved and new trees have just been planted.

Edward Treadwell

Incorporation, 1908

All in Burlingame had opinions about incorporation in early 1908. From the Country Club to the Woman's Club, to barbershops and poolrooms, incorporation was the topic of the day.

The *Burlingame Advance* took up the cause of incorporation. The Woman's Club, including some "hill residents," firmly supported it as a way of bringing order and regulation to an unkempt, unpaved town where it was all too easy to obtain alcoholic beverages. There was virtually no paving. Commuters often trudged through ankle-deep mud in total darkness or found their ways with the assistance of lanterns.

But many opposed incorporation. They believed the exactions of an incorporated city would be too great and felt that, if the community became a town, they would be robbed of the "country living" that had attracted them to Burlingame in the beginning.

The election was hotly fought. Women had not yet been granted the vote. Ninety men voted for incorporation; 83 opposed it. Burlingame became an official city on June 6, 1908.

Briefly, until city offices were moved to Weinberg Hall, the mayor and trustees met in the dental office of Dr. Ira H. Chapman, Burlingame's first dentist, in practice there since 1906.

Edward Treadwell, a noted attorney, was the first mayor. He remained a prominent town citizen until his death in 1955.

The photographer was looking north along San Mateo Drive when he took this photograph in 1911. Streets are still unpaved. Trolley tracks are at right; the Bank of Burlingame is at left.

Growing town with many problems

After the opening of the depot in 1894, people began to drift into Burlingame. In the year following the 1906 earthquake, they came in a flood.

Hundreds of lots were purchased in 1906 and 1907. The sound of hammers and saws reverberated through the community around the clock. Trustee Eric Lange noted that "there are no Sundays or holidays in Burlingame."

Life wasn't idyllic. Mosquitoes bred in the marsh at the Bay end of the town and swarmed through the business district. Commuters hurried to trains wearing netting around their faces, while the mosquitoes swarmed in black clouds.

Burlingame Avenue was a dirt road, flanked by towering eucalyptus trees. A few strips of isolated paving existed in front of some stores, otherwise there were no sidewalks. In winter, commuters trudged through ankle-deep mud.

Drainage constituted an ongoing and serious problem. Bay water at high tide often lapped across San Mateo Drive. Frequently, water was deep enough for town youngsters to sail their boats along the roadway.

Automobile travel

Automobile travel along the Peninsula began haltingly. Motor cars weren't welcomed in Burlingame where, it was noted in 1901, most drivers wantonly disregarded the rights of horses and pedestrians. One minister declared that no "chronic mobile driver" could also be a good Christian. Critics predicted that one day the infernal machines would cause fatal accidents.

As late as 1912, residents were still cautioned to drive below the posted 20 miles per hour. Ruts in County Road, many as deep as 16 inches, almost guaranteed broken springs, axles or both. Six miles per hour was the top speed considered safe.

Initial paving on County Road, undertaken for the Panama-Pacific International Exposition of 1915, began August 7, 1912. The inaugural stretch, a two-lane road, 24 feet wide, ran from South San Francisco to Burlingame. One-and-a-half inches of asphalt topped five inches of concrete.

An automobile party departs for an Independence Day celebration in 1912. Burlingame Stable was located on the southwest corner of Lorton and Donnelly avenues.

BURLINGAME HISTORICAL SOCIETY

BURLINGAME HISTORICAL SOCIETY

Tree-lined streets came to symbolize Burlingame even before the town was incorporated.

Weinberg Hall on Main Street served as the town's first city hall.

BURLINGAME HISTORICAL SOCIETY

Weinberg Hall

The venerable building was constructed on Main Street (Lorton) by Jacob and Rose Weinberg in 1908. In September 1910, town trustees refused to grant the couple a liquor license. Shortly thereafter, the couple was arrested and hauled into court for selling two quarts of illegal beer. Two weeks later Weinberg's was leased for use as Burlingame's first real city hall.

City offices were maintained there. It also was headquarters for the police. The fire bell, used to summon volunteers, was placed in front.

In 1910, Burlingame trustees allocated funds for a jail. They claimed it "looks well" for the city to have one. The two-cell lockup was purchased mail order from Milwaukee at a cost of $244. Some joked that people in town had clothes made by tailors but were willing to buy a jail from "a plebeian mail order house." The jail was installed in Weinberg Hall. The tax collector's office was on one side of the jail; the dog pound was behind it.

Aside from public meetings, Weinberg's also served as a place of worship. Eric Lange, an original town trustee, recalled that when one religious denomination filed out, another took its place. St. Catherine's Catholic and St. Paul's Episcopal were among the denominations to share space in the hall.

This landmark served the city until the opening of the new City Hall on Park Road in 1914.

Eric Lange

An American flag was donated to the
town by the Woman's Club in 1911.

Citizens made
Burlingame
a special place

The first of many annual fund raisers was staged
by the Burlingame Woman's Club in August 1907.
Indeed, the gala street carnival was described as a
"fairy frolic of music, confetti, fine gowns, candy and
laughter." Evening dancing under the glow of 1,600
Japanese lanterns was the chief attraction.

Profits from the carnival were earmarked for civic
improvement and beautification. The Woman's Club
worked to accomplish this mission with nothing short
of crusading zeal.

Construction of a safety station near the train
depot was high on the list of priorities. Such a shelter
would protect patrons awaiting pickup by the electric
trolley that rumbled through town every 20 minutes.
The safety station opened in 1908 and remained a
landmark for 30 years.

During the first two years of
club existence, more than 600
trees were planted along town
streets and in park sites. Club
members sponsored arbor days
when school children planted
trees. Neglected parks were
cleaned up and replanted.

"As long as we love, we serve,"
declared zealous women. They
ardently supported the public
library. In 1910, women erected a
mission bell on El Camino Real,
purchased another to call the
volunteer firemen and gave the
town its first official American flag.

*A trolley safety station headed the Woman's
Club agenda for civic betterment.*

BURLINGAME HISTORICAL SOCIETY

Early fire department

Fifteen volunteers gathered in 1907, the year before the town was incorporated, to form a fire department. They began without a single piece of equipment. Members paid dues and sponsored dances to raise funds.

After incorporation, town trustees approved a paltry $675 for purchase of a single four-wheeled chemical wagon. Although the department acquired a motorized truck in 1913, an unreliable Locomobile known as the "Never Ready," its first modern Seagrave pumper was purchased in 1922. Until 1929, there was no firehouse. Equipment was kept at the Dessin Brothers garage at Lorton and Donnelly.

Completion in 1929 of a downtown firehouse on California Drive marked a turning point in the department's history. The city agreed that, thereafter, the department should be organized with a few full-time firefighters.

The station, dedicated in 1930, provided room for equipment, an alarm system and workshops on the main floor. A social hall, kitchen and sleeping quarters were on the second.

Wilkie J. Dessin, a department legend, became a volunteer in 1912 and chief three years later. In addition to running the department, Dessin operated the town's Dodge automobile agency. He was injured at Washington School in 1940 when an explosion hurled him across a room. He never fully recovered and died two years later.

BURLINGAME HISTORICAL SOCIETY

The department's Seagrave hook and ladder truck was photographed at Oxford and Cambridge roads, March 1939. The photo became a mural at the Golden Gate International Exposition on Treasure Island.

BURLINGAME FIRE DEPARTMENT

Burlingame's first pumper on Donnelly Avenue in front of Dessin's Garage where it was housed.

37

In early Burlingame, muddy streets, such as these at Bellevue Avenue and San Mateo Drive in 1908, constituted a greater hazard than speeding cars.

BURLINGAME PUBLIC LIBRARY

BURLINGAME HISTORICAL SOCIETY

George E. Jones

Early town police department

During its formative years, a Burlingame without George E. Jones is almost inconceivable. Although a San Francisco native (b. 1869), he nevertheless had roots planted on the Peninsula. He attended St. Matthew's Military School during the 1870s and 1880s when it was still located in San Mateo (adjacent to St. Matthew's Episcopal Church).

Burlingame's first Board of Trustees appointed Jones the Superintendent of Streets, License and Tax Collector, Health Officer, Truant Officer and Chief of Police. If required, he also served as prosecutor. Those troubled by a loose dog or obnoxious cow called Jones.

Police Department headquarters was on the ground floor of Weinberg Hall. Previously, Jones had held the title Marshal. By 1915, his department had grown to three. The *Burlingame Advance* reported in September that town trustees had determined that the three men should be uniformed and wear "the same color and pattern regardless of complexions or approval by the wearers." The "natty new uniforms" were made of a "drab material with caps to match." Townsfolk concluded that the uniforms were in keeping with the "Burlingame Beautiful" idea.

The Burlingame Masonic Lodge's first officers were installed at San Mateo's Peninsula Hotel in October 1908.

Burlingame Masonic Lodge No. 400

In the waiting room of the Southern Pacific depot, March 15, 1908, Peninsula Masons gathered to speak in favor of forming a Burlingame lodge. Installation of original officers took place, in ceremony, at San Mateo's Peninsula Hotel, October 24, 1908. Thenceforth, the Masons met in Weinberg Hall on Burlingame's Main Street.

A cornerstone was laid for the Masonic temple in 1909. This Burlingame Avenue building, later known as the Arcade, subsequently sold to the Independent Order of Odd Fellows. A second temple, a $180,000 undertaking, at Howard Avenue and Park Road commenced in 1926 and was dedicated October 22, 1927.

Subscribing to high ideals, while delighting in secrecy and ritual, the Masons were America's largest fraternal order. This was a worldwide organization that had grown out of the guilds of stone workers who built Europe's medieval cathedrals. Masons described their order as "a system of morality based on allegory and illustrated symbols."

Fourteen American presidents had been Masons. Members represented all religions. At the height of Freemasonry's popularity after World War II, there were almost 1,500 Burlingame members. By the 1990s, the number had fallen to 600.

Ground was broken for Burlingame's first Masonic lodge in 1909. The Burlingame Avenue structure later housed the Independent Order of Odd Fellows.

St. Paul's Episcopal Church on El Camino Real opened in 1927.

City of churches

Churches became a point of civic pride. The town's oldest congregation, the First Baptist Church, met in the waiting room of the Southern Pacific depot in July 1906. A tiny church opened two years later and an elegant house of worship on Palm Drive near El Camino Real was dedicated November 23, 1930.

Christian Scientists met in the Masonic Hall on Burlingame Avenue in 1910 to form the First Church of Christ Scientist. The Methodist Church, located at Burlingame Avenue and Primrose, opened in 1908. The First Presbyterian Church formed in 1926. For two years the congregation met at Roosevelt School before occupying a new church at Easton near El Camino. St. Paul's Episcopal formed as a mission in Weinberg Hall the year the town was incorporated. Its rose-colored, English-style Gothic church at 415 El Camino was completed in 1927.

St. Catherine's Catholic also met at Weinberg Hall. Its first building, at the northeast corner of Park Road and Howard Avenue, was initially used in 1909. Our Lady of Angels Catholic occupied a portion of the old Easton Grammar School, organized as a parish in 1926.

The Lutheran Church of the Good Shepherd was established in the American Legion Hall in 1946 before moving to the Avenue. Trinity Lutheran was established.

Peninsula Temple Shalom, Burlingame's first Jewish synagogue, dated from 1955.

The Methodist Episcopal Church of 1908 ultimately was moved and became the United Methodist Church.

Bank of Burlingame, located at the corner of San Mateo Drive and Burlingame Avenue, opened in 1909. The tall structure is the Masonic Hall.

BURLINGAME HISTORICAL SOCIETY

Bank of Burlingame

Bank of Burlingame, designed by architect William H. Weeks, was organized in 1907. Its new building, completed in 1909 on the Square, was considered the town's most elegant structure. The two-story, reinforced concrete building was faced with Colusa stone.

The structure housed many early businesses, including Burlingame Drug Co. and the real estate offices of Lyon & Hoag. Dentist Ira Chapman and physician A.L. Offield also maintained offices there. For a brief period, the public library was housed in a second floor room.

Bank of Burlingame was a most revered institution. Sitting on its board were local luminaries Joseph Levy and John Wisnom. Industrialist Henry T. Scott and banker A.P. Giannini were also directors.

In more modern times, the bank served as Nathan's Restaurant, itself an Avenue landmark for a dozen years until it closed in 1994. Owners of Cafe Marimba, which occupied the building thereafter, infuriated traditionalists by painting it a garish cobalt blue with terra cotta trim. Proprietors bowed to public demand and repainted it in tones of "sand and sage." The gesture wasn't enough to save business. Within a year, it gave way to yet another restaurant.

The building's classic historical integrity was violated in 1996 when its corner entrance was relocated.

Hill people of the Millionaire Colony dedicated their lives to relaxation and the pursuit of pleasure.

Hill people relax on the lawn at Del Monte. Standing (left to right) are Ethel Crocker, Daisy (Parrott) Payson and a woman believed to have been Agnes Poett Howard Bowie. Seated in light-colored suits are Capt. Albert H. Payson, William H. Crocker and Henry P. Bowie. The man on the left is unidentified.

Revolt of the hill people

The Burlingame Country Club, established in 1893 as a lavish rural retreat for the well-born of San Francisco, was the town's first important institution. Industrialist Joseph D. Grant had led the way by building a great house on the hill during the early 1890s. Other fashionable San Franciscans followed in his footsteps. William H. Crocker, son of the railroader, built a country estate on Forest View Avenue. Crocker's brother-in-law, André Poniatowski, moved into *Ski Farm*, dominating the heights. Architect A. Page Brown built a group of English-style homes, the so-called Country Club cottages, near Occidental.

For "hill people," mostly millionaires, in search of elegant isolation, the idea of a modernized, paved and regulated Burlingame was repugnant.

Incorporating themselves as an act of community self-defense seemed to be the answer. An election was held in April 1910. *Hillsborough*, commonly the "Millionaire Colony," broke from Burlingame and came into existence May 6, 1910.

Hillsborough's goal was rustic simplicity to be guaranteed by charter provisions, unique in Northern California. There were to be *no* businesses, *no* telegraph or express offices, *no* churches, and to assure the bucolic atmosphere, *no* sidewalks.

Studebaker buses replaced the streetcar in 1918.

RUDOLPH BRANAT

TOM GRAY

The Burlingame Railway Co. consisted of a single, battery-powered streetcar.

Easton electric car

The quaint, yellow electric streetcar first ran on Washington's Birthday, 1913.

Real estate entrepreneur Ansel Mills Easton began attracting buyers for his North Burlingame property following the 1906 earthquake. To accommodate buyers, a small station, Easton, later Broadway-Burlingame, was erected on the trolley and railroad line.

To promote sales, Easton had constructed an electric streetcar that ran from the station along California Drive to Carmelita, west to Cabrillo, north to Hillside and thence up the incline to Hillside Circle, a total of 8,850 feet.

This car, which alone constituted the Burlingame Railway, was silently propelled by 119 Edison Storage Batteries located beneath the seats. It was the ultimate in electric transportation.

Builders claimed the 26-passenger car moved at 23 miles per hour, 5 miles per hour on upgrades, but significantly slower when loaded. When full, the car seldom made it up Hillside.

Burlingame Railway was a money loser. Sunny Sundays, when picnickers came out in force, were most profitable. Weekdays, the motorman often made the trip alone. Easton discontinued service in 1918 when the electric car was replaced with Studebaker buses.

BURLINGAME HISTORICAL SOCIETY

Ansel Mills Easton

Burlingame School, completed early in 1906, was undamaged by the 1906 earthquake.

This photograph of Burlingame Grammar School was snapped on dedication day in 1913. It was also known as Oak Grove School and later McKinley School.

Schools in Burlingame

Until 1912, when the town opened its first school, Burlingame youngsters attended county schools. One, commonly called Burlingame School, was located on County Road at Peninsula Avenue. (This structure later became Peninsula Avenue School.)

The elegant Mission and Moorish structure had been built in 1906 before the earthquake at a cost of $30,000. It was the first reinforced concrete building in the county and the only public structure not damaged by the 1906 temblors. By September that year, three teachers were supervising 200 children.

Burlingame voters approved a school district in 1911 and the board was formed in January 1912.

A temporary building, described as the "little red school house" at Howard and Primrose avenues, was constructed by town trustee August Berg in 1912. This eight-room structure served as Burlingame's single school until 1913.

Oak Grove School, first known as Burlingame Grammar School, designed by architect William H. Weeks, was dedicated in September 1913. This building at Oak Grove and County Road (701 Paloma) was later renamed McKinley School. Additions and changes in its exterior, designed by Ernest Norberg, were undertaken in 1923.

Park Road City Hall, begun in 1913 and completed the following year, became the pride of the young community.

Park Road City Hall

Burlingame residents voted $25,000 for construction of the town's new City Hall in November 1913. The cornerstone, on Park Road just south of Burlingame Avenue, was laid the following month.

This solid-looking brick structure was designed by architect Charles Peter Weeks. Commentators declared it to be among the "most handsome public buildings in the state." One wing housed the fire department; the other served as the jail and police station.

Dedication was August 27, 1914. The building had been completed within $200 of the $25,000 bond issue voted by the people.

In addition to an assembly hall for meetings of town trustees and other public gatherings, there was space for the city engineer, registrar of voters, tax collector and other city offices.

This building served as the government seat until 1970.

Policemen marched past the City Hall as part of the funeral for John J. Harper, Chief of Police from 1923 to 1945.

This early scene of Roosevelt School and uncrowded streets created an idyllic image of Burlingame.

BURLINGAME HISTORICAL SOCIETY

Burlingame City Attorney John Davis

A *Better place to live*

Fashionable Burlingame was going to be a pleasant place to live. This became a fetish of town leaders after 1910. They already congratulated themselves on the law that year prohibiting children from being in the streets after 9:30 p.m. unless accompanied by parent or guardian.

Anti-dog forces gathered steam. City Attorney John Davis authored a law (1916), restricting the numbers of dogs that could be kept to two. This was later amended to allow more if all neighbors within 350 feet of the dog owner's property consented. (A dog was a dog, the law stated, if over three months of age. Puppies up to three months of age didn't count.)

The zealous Davis announced a determination to legislate a spotless town, free from obnoxious odors and irritating noises. Burning and burying of garbage, common and annoying practices, came to an end in 1924 when a law forbade both means of disposal.

Downtown parking was restricted to a single hour, and all parking after dark was prohibited.

Residents in 1929 banned signs atop buildings and garages in residential neighborhoods. Southern Pacific Railroad was advised of the town's anti-noise ordinance; use of steam whistles was outlawed.

Davis muzzled roosters and legislated against boisterous doves, cackling geese and other backyard critters. The number of chickens allowed in 1930 to any one person was limited to 25.

Kohl house became a mecca for well-to-do hill people who delighted gathering there for sport and refreshment.

Charles Frederick Kohl

Charles Frederick Kohl always listed his profession simply as a capitalist. The son of Capt. William Kohl of San Francisco's prestigious Alaska Commercial Company, he grew up in San Mateo. In 1911, young Kohl was shot by a family maid. He survived but was physically disabled and forever after an emotional wreck.

Kohl and his vivacious young wife occupied their elegant new Tudor-style mansion on Adeline Drive in 1914. They separated two years later.

Meanwhile, convinced that the demented maid planned to plug him again, Kohl sneaked off to Del Monte Lodge on the Monterey Peninsula. After breakfast November 23, 1921, he shot himself.

Some years later, young nuns at the Mercy Convent–the Kohl house became the convent in 1924–reported on unexplainable circumstances including visions, eerie sounds, an empty elevator going up and down, and the sound of a limping figure stalking about the locked billiard room.

Sisters whispered that Kohl's ghost was haunting their Tudor halls. Twice, priests were summoned to say Masses for the deceased Kohl in the hopes of calming his Protestant soul.

Efforts were unsuccessful. Unexplained occurrences allegedly continued. Kohl's spirit was not portrayed as the sick and wretched loser he had been, but as gentle "Freddie," socialite and arts patron.

Mr. and Mrs. Charles Frederick Kohl, photographed while aboard their Lake Tahoe yacht, circa 1913.

An entourage of Philadelphia officials and policemen accompanied America's most cherished relic to San Francisco.

SMITHSONIAN INSTITUTION

While displayed at the Pennsylvania Building of the Panama-Pacific International Exposition, the Liberty Bell was placed upon a priceless 200-year old Persian carpet.

Liberty Bell in Burlingame

Although the Liberty Bell was not scheduled to stop, patriotic pandemonium reigned in Burlingame the night of July 16, 1915, when the nation's most cherished relic, mounted on a flatcar, was pulled up the Peninsula. It was en route to be exhibited at the Panama-Pacific International Exposition.

At 11:30 p.m., the *Liberty Bell Special* came into view. Burlingame residents surged forward, forcing the engineer to slow almost to a stop. Hundreds lined the tracks.

In 1904, rough handling had worsened the crack in the bell while on tour in the South. Thereafter, Philadelphians vowed never to let it leave the city again, but heavy pressure from California had forced the change in policy.

A flatcar with special springs and shock absorbers to prevent jolting was constructed. American flags were posted on each corner of the car. Electric illumination was devised to bathe the Liberty Bell in light during darkness. It could be seen for half a mile. The Bell's official entourage included four Philadelphia policemen.

The Bell's return to Philadelphia began November 11, 1915. More crowds lined the tracks. After its return, the Liberty Bell never again left Philadelphia.

Commuting via buses of the Peninsula Rapid Transit Co. began in 1915.

RUDOLPH BRANDT

Peninsula Rapid Transit Company

Burlingame was a commuter's town. Augmenting train and trolley service, Peninsula Rapid Transit Company was established in 1915. Bus operations aboard 24-passenger enclosed cars began May 22, 1915. During its first week, the line struggled to deal with a more than capacity demand for service.

In pleasant weather, windows could be opened. Commuters agreed that the ride was equal in enjoyment to rides in silent, smooth-running touring cars. Buses were electrically lit and heated from the engine exhaust. Buses averaged 20 miles per hour.

The company ran sufficient numbers of buses to maintain a half-hourly service between San Mateo and San Francisco. The fare for the 60-minute ride was 25 cents. From San Mateo to Palo Alto, an hourly service, required another 30 minutes and an additional quarter. Fares between various parts of the line began at 5 cents. Rates were some of the least expensive in the United States. Cost per traveler was approximately one and a quarter cents per mile.

William H. Pearson of Burlingame became Peninsula Rapid Transit's president in 1915. He claimed that the company was a key factor in budding suburbia. Pearson remained at the helm of the company for 15 years.

Burlingame resident William H. Pearson headed the transit company for 15 years.

49

Howard Avenue School, later Washington, as it appeared when opened in 1915.

BURLINGAME HISTORICAL SOCIETY

Howard Avenue School

Howard Avenue School, designed by architect Ernest L. Norberg, opened as Burlingame's second grammar school in 1915. The two-story structure at 801 Howard was the largest in east Burlingame. At the conclusion of the Panama-Pacific International Exposition, in December 1915, school officials acquired Exposition playground equipment for use at the school. Howard Avenue was subsequently called Washington School (1940).

The town's ever-increasing population almost immediately made more schools a necessity. Roosevelt School, originally called Roosevelt Grammar School, opened (1151 Vancouver) in 1919, Pershing (1560 Newlands) in 1921, Coolidge (1400 Paloma) in 1926, Hoover (2220 Summit) in 1930, Lincoln (1801 Devereux) in 1950 and Franklin (2385 Trousdale) in 1958. Traditionally, last names only have been used.

Coolidge closed in 1972. Pershing, Hoover and Roosevelt were closed in the late 1970s because of declining enrollments. The board of trustees scheduled the re-opening of renovated Roosevelt School in September 1997. Both Pershing and Coolidge were torn down. Hoover was sold to become headquarters of Shinnyo-En Buddhism, the largest growing Buddhist sect outside Japan.

Burlingame Intermediate, the town's single intermediate institution, opened in spring 1953.

Burlingame Avenue's first motion picture show house was on the site of the old Gates house and opened in 1918.

Garden Theatre

Burlingame's first motion picture theater was George Roy's Photoplay (also known as The Roy), on San Mateo Drive, which opened May 15, 1913. Chairs were hard; films flickered and jumped. Patrons watched two-reel features for a nickel.

The Roy didn't survive the premier of the Garden Theatre, September 23, 1918. Designed by architect Ernest L. Norberg, it was located on the George W. Gates homesite on the north side of the Avenue a block from the depot.

Especially fine, the Garden was renowned for motion pictures and vaudeville productions. The lobby included a crackling fireplace. In the loges, wicker chairs added special comfort. Walls were decorated with hand-painted murals. Vincent's, a candy store and soda fountain, was located next door for the convenience of patrons.

The Garden continued to operate until 1925 when the imminent opening of the more luxurious Peninsula Theatre made it seem obsolete.

Vincent's candy shop was located next to the Garden Theatre for the convenience of customers.

One of the town's first professional women, Crawford sold many of her high society photographs to San Francisco newspapers.

SAN MATEO COUNTY HISTORICAL MUSEUM

Photographer to children and high society

Dorothy M. Crawford, born Maude Frink in Kansas (1877), moved to Burlingame in 1914. In an era long before workingwomen were considered acceptable, Crawford studied art and went to work as a photographer, a profession she passionately pursued until retiring in 1944. Crawford was recognized as one of Burlingame's first professional women.

Though she did pictures of streets, houses and landscapes, she referred to herself as a portrait photographer. Many of her pictures won state and national prizes; some were published nationally. She was best known for portraits of children.

Crawford once declared that there was no system to taking pictures of youngsters. Some children "are too quick for the camera." One of her young subjects sat through 25 sittings before Crawford got four images she liked.

Society matrons of Hillsborough held special appreciation for her talent. Many of her high society photographs found their way to the social pages of the *Chronicle*, *Call* and *Examiner*, San Francisco's leading newspapers.

Dorothy Crawford took this portrait of (left to right) Ray, Ed and Francis Arnold, probably in 1917.

ED ARNOLD

52

Auto Row

There were streetcars and trains. In theory, automobiles in Burlingame weren't necessary. Yet, there seemed to be more cars buzzing about the town than anywhere else on the Peninsula.

Some said it was because of the opulence of nearby Hillsborough. In any case, as early as 1918, Burlingame was already the automobile center of the Peninsula and regarded as the ideal location for opening dealerships.

The *Burlingame Advance* first used the term "Auto Row" in 1923. During the early 1920s, Dodge, Ford and Lincoln dealers opened showrooms on Lorton Avenue. Levy Bros. operated a Buick showroom.

Herbert Vielbaum opened Pacific Auto Repair on San Mateo Drive in 1921. This long-lived business was an important link in the automobile servicing chain.

The halcyon days of the dealerships were tarnished during the Depression and World War II. Prosperity resurged after the war. Many dealers came and went, but a few became standard fixtures. Rector Cadillac opened in 1953 and Mike Harvey established himself in 1971.

This racing car was rebuilt (1912) by Wilkie J. Dessin for Bill Boulding.

Dessin Bros. Garage as it was photographed n 1921.

Police Chief Jack Theuer (left) and policeman Lawrence Furio accepting a new Dodge squad car during the 1950s

SISTERS OF MERCY

The Kohl mansion gave North Burlingame a flavor of Elizabethan England.

SISTERS OF MERCY

Kohl's Great Hall was the scene of numerous organ concerts during the builder's tenure there.

Mrs. Charles Frederick Kohl (right) was an avid devotee of "beagling," the sport of pursuing jackrabbits with packs of hounds.

Kohl Mansion

Charles Frederick Kohl's red-brick Tudor mansion, nestled amid 40 acres of gnarled oaks, was erected along Adeline Drive in 1914. The $525,000 structure became known for 42,000 feet of floor space, high gabled roof, brick facade and a great hall measuring 27 by 60 feet. With a flavor of Elizabethan England, it is one of last great Tudors constructed in San Mateo County.

Kohl died in 1921. Three years later the house and property sold to the Sisters of Mercy for $230,000. For almost a decade, it served as a convent for the Sisters of Mercy. In 1932, it became Mercy High School, a private Roman Catholic educational institution for girls.

*Mary Pickford and
Douglas Fairbanks*

*While the story was criticized, all agreed
that the setting was "strikingly beautiful."*

Mary Pickford was the "Little Lord"

Mary and Doug, a flock of sheep, horses galore, a 160-pound St. Bernard named "Sport," and a passel of flunkies and supernumeraries swooped down on North Burlingame in July 1921.

Mary was "America's Sweetheart," charming Mary Pickford. Doug was her film-hero husband Douglas Fairbanks. Burlingame was the location for filming the super-production, "Little Lord Fauntleroy." United Artists wanted to shoot the film in England. But after viewing photos of Peninsula estates, they chose the North Burlingame home of C. Frederick Kohl.

Pickford pronounced the mansion, surrounded by ancient oaks and formal English gardens, a perfect replica of Dorincourt Castle, setting for Frances Hodgson Burnett's tale of an American boy who became an English lord (1886).

This was film history. Pickford appeared both as the little lord and as his mother. Audiences were flabbergasted at the film magic, namely the apparent difference in height between Mary the mother and Mary the boy. In one three-second segment, Mary (mother) kisses Mary (son). It took 16 hours to shoot.

Critics declared that "Fauntleroy" included some of the best photography ever put to screen. Settings "delighted the eye" and location shots were "strikingly beautiful."

*Mary Pickford as the "Little Lord."
Critics said she wasn't convincing.*

Well-dressed crowds mobbed Pacific City to promenade along the boardwalk during the amusement park's inaugural year.

An imposing entry portended a prosperity that never materialized.

Boosters touted the roller coaster as having been the world's steepest.

Pacific City

Pacific City, a grand amusement park touted as the "greatest fun community since the creation of Coney Island," opened at Coyote Point at the foot of Peninsula Avenue, July 1, 1922.

Burlingame, San Mateo and Hillsborough boosters predicted that their towns would become resorts rivaling the great ones of Southern California. Pacific City, officially in San Mateo, was centered on a 3,200-foot boardwalk stretching along a mile of sandy beach. A pier accommodated excursion boats. Visitors marveled at the soft white sand, not realizing that 2,000 tons of it had been trucked in from Monterey beaches.

It was a youngster's paradise. There was a monster roller coaster and traditional rides. A one-time Navy training ship was towed ashore and transformed into a 500-seat restaurant.

Pacific City never succeeded as a resort, in part because adequate transportation from San Francisco to Burlingame was never developed and backers couldn't control bone-chilling winds.

A second season began in 1923. But cool weather accompanied by a foul stench caused by Burlingame's sewer system, emptying into the Bay, also kept crowds small. Health officials forbade swimming. The enterprise went bankrupt by the season's end.

RUDOLPH BRANDT

A 1923 Hupmobile leaves Burlingame, driving north on El Camino Real.

Pillars of Burlingame

Determined to advertise the town of Burlingame when the State Highway (El Camino Real) was being paved in 1912, millionaire architect George H. Howard Jr. drew plans for ornamental pillars to be placed at the north and south entrances to Burlingame, to mark the then energetic and rapidly growing city.

Four stone pillars, each weighing approximately 30 tons, were constructed. Then, automobile speeds averaged 10 to 12 miles per hour.

Faster speeds along the highway soon resulted in accidents. Ultimately, four motorists were killed in crashes with what the press termed Burlingame's "death gates."

Nevertheless, town trustees hesitated to order their removal. Finally, in 1923, the San Mateo County Board of Supervisors settled the problem. The pillars were doomed.

Burlingame Police Chief Lewis A. Cavalier was saddened by the order. He declared that the gates served as his "most faithful officers" and predicted more motorists would now be killed because of higher speeds on the Peninsula's only highway.

RUDOLPH BRANDT

Entry to and exit from Burlingame along El Camino Real was marked by pillars. The southern pillars were at Peninsula Avenue.

57

Architect Harry A. Thomsen builds unique home

Harry A. Thomsen

Architect Harry A. Thomsen built his home at 1617 Chapin in the early 1920s. The house, along with the original rosebush planted in front, still exists. The rose never fails to bloom.

Thomsen, first employed as an assistant and then as partner of famed architect George Kellan, took part in the reconstruction of the Palace Hotel in San Francisco following the 1906 earthquake. Thomsen eventually took over the firm. Later, it became Thomsen and Wilson.

Some of Thomsen's better known San Francisco works include the Russ, Shell and Standard Oil buildings. He was a consultant on both the Wells Fargo and Bank of America buildings. He designed many buildings for the University of California (Berkeley) and the University of California, Los Angeles.

Following World War II, Thomsen employed 130 architects and had scores of projects underway simultaneously.

Thomsen designed the house on Chapin. His daughter, Barbara, who grew up there, recalled that it was built on two lots and included four bedrooms and two baths in addition to a sleeping porch. Rooms were known for Italian simplicity and redwood beamed ceilings. Below the stairs on the first floor were a safe, a liquor closet and a telephone. Thomsen had wood for the front door buried to age it properly before use.

The Chapin house was an architectural marvel. An article about it was included in the *Pacific Coast Architect* of October 1924.

The Thomsen home was noted for beamed ceilings and unique architectural design.

Thomsen designed and built his own house on Chapin Avenue.

58

United Methodist Church

Movement of the Methodist Church, in May 1924, from its original location at the southeast corner of Burlingame Avenue and Primrose Road to its new site at Howard Avenue and El Camino Real was choreographed with military precision.

The building, which opened as the Methodist Episcopal Church June 1908, was moved to make way for Levy Bros. Department Store. The one block move along Primrose wasn't traversed without difficulty. In fact, town trustees even suggested cutting the structure in half to minimize the task. Church fathers objected, claiming it could be moved in one piece if trees along Primrose were removed.

The church was placed on rollers. A zigzag route was plotted. Knowing that Primrose residents opposed tree cutting, crews of axe-wielding cutters were assigned to *each* tree. At the toot of a whistle all stalks were to be sliced simultaneously.

It almost worked. Small trees fell instantly. One, entangled in electric wires couldn't be cut. No one counted on Carol Stoner who threw her arms around a tree trunk, challenging men to "chop through me first." E.F. Gould protected his tree with a shotgun.

War was averted when Father James Grant of St. Catherine's Church, whose parish house was on the east side of Primrose, decided that trees on his property should be "trimmed," while allowing that bending them "slightly" would do no permanent harm.

The new church was dedicated February 15, 1925.

The Methodist Episcopal Church on Burlingame Avenue and Primrose Road as it appeared while under construction in 1908.

The United Methodist Church, a town landmark, has been at El Camino Real and Howard Avenue since 1924.

Sisters of Mercy

Mercy novices, during the late 1920s, were identified by their white muslin veils.

Entering postulants in 1928 are posed against the vine-covered Mercy convent.

The Sisters of Mercy were drawn to *The Oaks*, the late C. Frederick Kohl's 63-room mansion, by a brochure portraying it as ideal for "some educational religious order" picturing nuns walking among its oaks and roses. It was halfway up unpaved Adeline Drive.

Nuns arrived in February 1924. Early the next year, shouting Ku Klux Klansmen, opposed to "Negroes, Jews and Roman Catholics" encircled the convent. Shots were fired. A cross burned across the canyon.

Under the nuns' tenure, Kohl elegance disappeared. Bedrooms became dormitories for six to eight nuns each. Satin covered walls were painted stark white. Curtains created individual cells.

Silence was observed whenever possible. Talking at mealtime was forbidden. Novices were awakened at 4:50 a.m. and the day ended at 9:30 p.m. No one spoke at night. Visits into town weren't allowed. Girls remained on the property for two full years. Tradition had it that if a girl took a single step outside, she would have to begin her studies anew. Others believed that if they left the property, they'd be sent home—the ultimate disgrace.

Kohl house remained the convent until 1931. In those seven years, 71 girls entered; eight were sent home. After 1931, the convent was moved to other buildings on the grounds.

Sisters of Mercy wore black woolen neck-to-floor habits with black leather belts. A rosary of large beads with a crucifix was worn on the right side.

Non-Caucasians were required to be off the streets by sundown and were restricted from owning property. Sotero Aboy went to work as a chauffeur for the R.R. Strange family about 1920. This photo was snapped several years later.

Burlingame strives to be a white town

"Tell your parents we want to keep this a white town," Burlingame High School's Edward Hevey told his classes in the 1950s.

Hevey, who, in addition to being a teacher, sold real estate, was echoing the wishes of city fathers. As late as 1947, those purchasing property agreed that lots "shall not, nor shall any part thereof...be occupied by any person or persons other than those of the Caucasian or white race."

Old land deeds continued to carry such restrictions, but after the 1950s, they no longer had validity. Such clauses were omitted from new deeds.

The only non-whites allowed to reside in the city of Burlingame were those who held positions of servitude. Early law required that non-Caucasians be off the streets by sunset.

By the 1930s, Burlingame Avenue, looking toward the depot, no longer had the characteristics of an unsophisticated village.

Forsythe & Simpson, a men's shop at 1294 Burlingame, as it appeared in 1927, after moving from a smaller store.

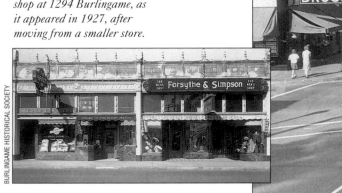

BURLINGAME HISTORICAL SOCIETY

BURLINGAME HISTORICAL SOCIETY

Proud John Forsythe and David Simpson display their wares at their men's shop at 1207 Burlingame Avenue. The photo was taken in 1926; they moved the following year.

Burlingame Avenue

"Hill people" (as residents of west Burlingame who later incorporated the town of Hillsborough were known) insisted upon calling Burlingame the *Village* and the street which ran west from the railroad station the *Avenue*.

In 1906, at the time of the earthquake, town population had been 200. By 1916, population had skyrocketed past 4,000. Burlingame's population by 1925, 11,170, made it the largest city in San Mateo County. As early as 1920, more commuters left Burlingame station per day than any other stop between San Francisco and San Jose.

From the time of incorporation in 1908, town citizens had dedicated themselves to making the Avenue the handsomest business street on the Peninsula. Not only was it paved, but sidewalks were installed.

The Avenue's big year was 1924 when it experienced unparalleled development. Buildings were occupied as fast as they could be constructed.

Morgan Gunst (son of Moses Gunst), owner of a home in what became Washington Park, paid $40,000 for a lot at Burlingame Avenue and Primrose (1924). Several months later, he sold for $50,000 or $500 per square foot, the highest price ever paid for Peninsula property to that time.

The Lorton and Rehe Building was erected in 1924. It later housed the Burlingame Hotel.

Built in Mission Revival style, the grocery and hardware store on the southwest corner of Lorton and Burlingame avenues was one of the original downtown businesses.

Frederick Lorton & Rehe Building

Burlingame schools closed, shopping was delayed and business was suspended August 28, 1924. Young and old alike gathered at the intersection of Burlingame Avenue and Middlefield (later Lorton) to watch a steam shovel begin excavating the southwest corner for the foundation of the Lorton & Rehe Building. The mammoth steam-belching shovel, first of its kind used on the Peninsula, was a source of fascination.

This new three-story, reinforced concrete building, commissioned by real estate and insurance men Frederick D. Lorton and John Rehe, housed five stores on the ground floor. Upstairs was reserved for offices and apartments.

The corner had been the site of Burlingame Avenue's first building dating from 1906. It had housed the Burlingame Grocery and Hardware Company along with Schmidt's Meat Market.

John Bromfield became manager of Levy Bros. in 1924.

Levy Bros.

This department store traced its San Mateo County existence to Half Moon Bay (1872), when Fernand and Joseph Levy, French-speaking sons of a Jewish storekeeper from Alsace-Loraine, opened a general store. Later they were joined by brothers Adrien and Armand. Their first Burlingame store on the Avenue dated from 1920.

In 1924, the company acquired the land at the corner of Burlingame Avenue and Primrose, the site of the town's Methodist Church. Subsequently, the church was moved to Howard Avenue and El Camino Real. Levy Bros. began construction of a pretentious, more fashionable reinforced concrete store of distinct Spanish Renaissance styling in October. Designed by architect Ernest Norberg, it opened May 1, 1925.

The Burlingame Avenue entrance was highlighted by an imposing arcade vestibule and stone Corinthian columns forming a vaulting ceiling. Architectural critics agreed that the building showed "thought and study" while indicating "an honest effort to depart from...hackneyed easy-to-do department store buildings."

Manager John D. Bromfield declared that the store would feature groceries, fresh meat, a delicatessen, fruits and vegetables, a bakery, tobacco, candy, stationery, dry goods, men's furnishings, hardware, building supplies, shoes, books and a beauty parlor.

The store, a $200,000 investment, specialized in expensive items designed to attract the area's fashionable set.

Levy Bros. department store was designed by architect Ernest L. Norberg and was considered one of his signature buildings.

St. Catherine's became the Catholic Church for both Burlingame and Hillsborough, the latter a town without churches.

St. Catherine's altar boys were photographed in May 1923. Back row (left to right) are: Edward Ferrara, Oswald Cooks, Francis Bakewell and Harry Sullivan. In the front row: Ed Bakewell, Aldo Ferrara, Francis Thompson and Edgar Arnold.

Saint Catherine of Siena Church

Saint Catherine of Siena, Burlingame's Roman Catholic parish, was created by San Francisco's Archbishop Patrick W. Riordan in August 1908. Boundaries extended from Poplar Avenue in San Mateo to the San Francisco line. The church served two missions in San Bruno and Millbrae. Both were established in 1909.

Father James A. Grant, a Scotsman, celebrated the parish's first Mass (September 14, 1908) at Weinberg Hall, a public gathering place on Main Street (later Lorton).

A year after establishment, a church was completed on the northeast corner of Park Road and Howard Avenue. Riordan celebrated Mass there October 3, 1909.

Fifteen years later, land was acquired at Bayswater Avenue and Primrose Road. In August 1925, both rectory and church were moved there at a cost of $35,000. During that upheaval, Masses were said in the Burlingame High School auditorium.

A new church was erected on the same site and dedicated September 7, 1952. The nave of this traditional English Gothic-style edifice was 70 feet high. The tower rose to 110 feet.

Designed to serve Catholics in Burlingame and Hillsborough (where no churches existed), the church had a capacity of 900.

The facade and spire of St. Catherine's were easily recognizable characteristics of the Catholic Church.

Town with a bad reputation... motorists beware

One Sunday in 1921, more than 20,000 automobiles passed along the State Highway (El Camino Real) in Burlingame. A study by the automobile association noted that a car passed a given point every two and one-half seconds over a 14-hour period.

Residents argued about law enforcement. Hundreds of motorists were cited daily for speeding violations and hauled into Burlingame City Hall for fine or release.

It appeared that town fathers were relentlessly waging war against motorists. Residents resented the notoriety when, in fact, the crackdown was conducted by the State of California. Cops, herding miscreants into Burlingame should cease and desist, declared public relations-conscious Burlingame residents.

State officials summarily dismissed these concerns. City trustees finally told Burlingame Justice of the Peace Walter M. Bird he could no longer use the City Hall courtroom.

A bad move. On February 6, 1925, escorted by state policemen, sirens howling, he drove up to Burlingame City Hall. "Hear ye, hear ye," bellowed Bird. "Court is now in session," right out on Park Road under the trees.

Those who snickered were threatened with contempt and jail. Bird went through 18 of 57 cases on his docket. Burlingame trustees, to their embarrassment, revoked the eviction order.

Cars speeding along the newly paved El Camino Real in 1915.

*The Moses Gunst home on
Burlingame Avenue was
located in what became
Washington Park.*

BURLINGAME HISTORICAL SOCIETY

Moses Gunst Estate

Moses A. Gunst, born July 4, 1853, embodied a saga of American achievement. Admirers declared that no local citizen could shake hands with more men as intimate friends than Gunst. He hobnobbed with the famous and the great. Even Theodore Roosevelt was a confidant.

Gunst maintained a 17-room vacation home, a stuccoed structure, on 7.3 acres at 900 Burlingame Ave. His property later became Washington Park.

Cigars had made him rich. Two New York importers notwithstanding, by 1887 Gunst was America's leading cigar vendor. He imported four million cigars a year, mostly from Cuba. As many as 5,000 boxes of cigars a month were shipped to the East.

As a San Francisco Police Commissioner, he was progressive and, during eight turbulent years, always in the eye of controversy. Gunst thundered that police officers were untidy, sloppy and a sorry picture.

Gunst was Burlingame's most prominent Jew. Following World War I, as chairman of the American Jewish Relief Committee, he raised almost $4 million for the organization.

He died in Burlingame in 1928. He was 75.

MARY JANE CLINTON

*Moses Gunst (left), a San Francisco
Police Commissioner, was photographed
in 1887 with fellow commissioners
William Alvord, Police Chief Patrick
Crowley and Robert Tobin.*

BURLINGAME HISTORICAL SOCIETY

*Burlingame High School
opened in 1923.*

Burlingame High School

BURLINGAME HISTORICAL SOCIETY

*A portion of Burlingame High School
graduates, in January 1929, demonstrate
student fashion and hairstyles on the eve of
the Great Depression.*

In 1923, its first year, 419 students attended the high school. There were 30 teachers. The inscription on the building read: "San Mateo High School-Burlingame Branch." Burlingame High School did not become an independent institution until 1928. It was built to accommodate 1,500 students.

Land for the school, at 400 Carolan Avenue, formerly part of Corbitt-Carolan property, was purchased in 1921. The ultra-modern building, designed by architect William H. Weeks, was constructed at a cost of $300,000. A gymnasium, designed by Ernest L. Norberg, was added in 1928.

Students during the 1920s adopted the colors *red* and *white*. Their mascot was the panther and the motto selected was "Not the Biggest but the Best." Sports, pep rallies and bonfires dominated extra-curricular activities.

Students from San Bruno, Lomita Park and Millbrae swelled the size of the student body. Most came via the trolley. Commute tickets, bought through the school office, made the price of a round trip seven cents.

BURLINGAME HISTORICAL SOCIETY

William H. Crocker surrounded by his admirers on a regular ride through Burlingame.

Burlingame's most popular non-resident

Although a resident of Hillsborough, banker-millionaire William H. Crocker, youngest son of the transcontinental railroad builder, was for years a most popular man in Burlingame. Crocker built a Burlingame home in the 1890s and came to live permanently after the 1906 earthquake. Crocker became one of the founders of Hillsborough in 1910.

Weekdays he rode horseback from *New Place*, his 500-acre estate, to the Burlingame depot for his commute to San Francisco. Much to the delight of town youngsters, he kept his pockets full of coins, which he dispensed freely. His comings were always eagerly awaited. (A Crocker servant would always follow him in an automobile to the station. When Crocker boarded the train, the horse's reigns were attached to the back bumper of the car and the horse was trotted back to his stable.)

During the 1930s, after the death of his wife, Crocker also became a regular evening visitor, often five nights a week, both to San Mateo and Burlingame to attend the movies. For him to see the same film three or four times wasn't unusual. The manager of the Peninsula Theater would anticipate his arrival. The center seat in the first row of the balcony was reserved for the popular banker.

BURLINGAME HISTORICAL SOCIETY

Burlingame's Betty Daly got a special treat when Crocker offered her a ride with him.

Harry L. Miller opened Miller Drug Co. in 1906. It became a town landmark.

BURLINGAME HISTORICAL SOCIETY

BURLINGAME HISTORICAL SOCIETY

Miller Drug Co. on the Avenue was noted for its variety of merchandise during and after World War I.

Miller Drug Company

Shortly after the earthquake in 1906, Harry L. Miller established the Miller Drug Co. on San Mateo Drive in Burlingame Square. Seven years later, with the beginning of Avenue development, he moved the business to a one-story, frame building on the northwest corner of Burlingame and Lorton avenues.

Miller Drugs kept pace with town growth. In 1922, Miller established a second drugstore on Broadway. The original store occupied a new $50,000 Commercial Building on the Avenue in 1927.

Even so, three years later, at a cost of $7,000, Miller undertook a complete renovation. The renovated store included a soda fountain, finished with inlaid tile and elegant showcases.

Fountain service was instituted September 6, 1930. It included salads, sandwiches and soft drinks. Such had been deemed necessary to give complete accommodation to customers. A novel aspect of the store was a huge display window, incorporating 30-foot frontage on the Avenue and 70 feet on Lorton.

Burlingame High's marching band was a prize winning organization during the 1950s.

A Burlingame High football team, during the 1920s, proudly poses in front of the gymnasium.

San Mateo–Burlingame football

There was no greater football rivalry than the annual blood match between the Burlingame Panthers and the San Mateo Bearcats. The *Little Big Game* wasn't for the faint of heart. During the 1920s, the Armistice Day event was always played on Burlingame High School field. It seemed the whole of both towns showed up.

For days before, rooters on both sides surreptitiously gathered rotten eggs, tomatoes and wilted vegetables. Burlingame police stopped suspicious cars entering town to confiscate such weapons. San Mateo students were often jailed. Shenanigans became increasingly fierce. In 1935, authorities canceled the game because of rioting the previous season.

The game itself was always an anti-climax. After the final gun, screaming students from both sides would climb atop cars and onto running boards to ride up and down the Avenue. Burlingame rooters wore the traditional red and white; San Mateans stuck with black and orange.

Brick Mitchell (right) was the popular Burlingame coach in the 1920s.

Residents in the area of El Camino Real and Broadway were less than happy with the horn-operated signal installed at the intersection in 1929.

Progressive town:
Traffic control by horn blowing

American City Magazine in March 1929, sang the praises of Burlingame as a progressive residential community with agonizing traffic problems, especially on holidays and weekends. Traffic along El Camino Real was constant. The standard traffic light at Broadway caused nightmarish jams.

Town officials declared that a standard automatic signal timer wasn't workable. A newfangled signal, the first of its type in California, was installed. Vehicular traffic approaching the highway from Broadway, faced with a red light, stopped next to a sound-collecting box at the right curb, sounded horns and the green light appeared. Highway traffic stopped.

The traffic-operated control also provided for pedestrian crossing by means of a button located at the side of the crosswalk. The button performed the same service for pedestrians as did the sound-collector for the automobilist.

The traffic signal at El Camino Real and Broadway created a genuine bottleneck during the 1920s.

Pershing School was looked upon as one of Norberg's more beautiful creations when it opened in 1921.

BURLINGAME HISTORICAL SOCIETY

Architect Ernest L. Norberg

No person left a greater imprint on the community's architectural personality than did Ernest Louis Norberg who maintained offices in both San Francisco and Burlingame.

A native of Omaha (b. 1890), Norberg became a local resident in 1907. He received architectural training at San Francisco's Hopkins Art Institute. He served 32 years in the Army and, thereafter, was always known as Col. Norberg.

He worked with architect Willis Polk, designing both the Hobart building in San Francisco and *Uplands*, a Hillsborough mansion for C. Templeton Crocker (since 1950s, Crystal Springs and Crystal Springs Uplands schools). His architectural signature was his use of columns in building facades. He designed the Burlingame Public Library, Levy Bros. (later Crosby Commons), San Mateo High School, and both Washington and Pershing schools in Burlingame. Norberg was a charter member of the American Institute of Architects. He lived in Burlingame for 72 years and was *Citizen of the Year* in 1976. Norberg died in 1979.

BURLINGAME PUBLIC LIBRARY

Ernest L. Norberg

Ernest Norberg designed the library that opened on Primrose in 1930.

Elegance characterized the Burlingame Public Library located on Primrose, it was a recognized center of the community after 1930.

BURLINGAME PUBLIC LIBRARY

BURLINGAME HISTORICAL SOCIETY

BURLINGAME HISTORICAL SOCIETY

The old Congregational Church served as the public library between 1912 and 1930.

Burlingame Public Library

Trustees created a public library October 18, 1909, and Mrs. George E. Jones, wife of the town marshal, was the librarian. The library's initial home was on the second floor of the Burlingame Bank Building at the corner of the Avenue and San Mateo Drive. Thereafter, for a short time, the library was moved to a partitioned portion of Weinberg Hall.

On July 7, 1912, the library, in need of additional space, took over the building constructed in 1907 as Burlingame's First Congregational Church at Primrose and Bellevue. After the church disbanded, the city purchased the structure for $3,000.

A children's reading room was added in 1915. For years, old-timers tenderly recalled children's story hours held Saturday mornings on the lawn.

Burlingame architect Ernest L. Norberg, was directed in 1929 to create plans for a new library at a cost not to exceed $65,000. Work on the building began in September 1930. It opened to the public April 6, 1931.

Far too small to provide effective service, during the 1990s, the building was razed and a much enlarged structure constructed on the same site. The new $13 million facility, which opened in fall 1997, maintained the original reading and reference room along with architect Norberg's original facade.

Mercy High School

Mercy High School opened in the former Kohl mansion on Adeline Drive in 1931. Thirty-six girls were admitted to the first class. Under the auspices of the Sisters of Mercy, the school was started as an expression of the order's mission to educate girls from a variety of social and economic backgrounds. During its early decades, the school became noted for the high quality of its musical education. The first graduates received their diplomas in 1934.

Marie Haff, a member of the original graduating class recalled that "there was no swimming pool and there were no tennis courts. Our gym was a converted garage, and we exercised in black bloomers and middy blouses, and that was before showers were installed."

Initially, day-to-day uniforms were navy blue serge skirts and jackets with ivory blouses, blue ties, long cotton stockings and saddle oxfords. Few complained of being cold.

A classroom wing was added to the old mansion in 1955 and a swimming pool and athletic building were completed in 1959.

While during the school's early decades few graduates attended college, in later years the number has risen. Since 1980, between 90 and 100 percent of each class has advanced to higher education.

Many former students report that for them, four years at Mercy was more than mere schooling; it was a way of life.

On the Peninsula, Mercy High School helped pioneer the idea of higher education for women.

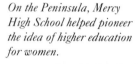

SISTERS OF MERCY

SISTERS OF MERCY

Grace culture classes at Mercy High School were a combination of calisthenics and dance.

SISTERS OF MERCY

Mercy High School's library was set up in what had been the Kohl dining room.

*Beginning in the 1920s,
Burlingame baseball
games were played in
Washington Park.*

Washington Park

*Washington Park, so dedicated in
1932, became known for its wide
variety of trees.*

By a vote of nearly eight to one, residents of Burlingame, in December 1921, voted in favor of a public park through the purchase of 10 acres of one-time *Crossways Farm*, adjacent to the high school.

The year 1932 was an important one in America. February 22 marked the bicentennial of George Washington's birth. In Burlingame, the event was celebrated with the rededication of the city park in memory of the nation's first president. An ordinance renaming the park for Washington was read by City Attorney John Davis. Representatives of the Woman's Auxiliary of the American Legion, the Burlingame Chapter of the Daughters of the American Revolution and the Burlingame Woman's Club planted three *sequoia sempervirens*, coast redwood trees.

Patriotic songs were sung and poems recited. Preceding the ceremonies at the park, one of the most colorful parades in Burlingame history traversed the Avenue. Practically every organization in town participated.

Massed colors at the park were presented by every American Legion post in the county. There were units from Burlingame, San Mateo, Belmont, Redwood City, Daly City and Menlo Park.

JUN 29 1932

BLOCK NEWS
VOL. I NO. I

NEIGHBORHOOD NEWS
2¢ a paper
5¢ a month
CIRCULATION
25 copies
VOL I NO. 5   PAGE I

Readers of the Neighborhood News wanted to believe that it was a publication exclusively done by local children.

Billy George and Bobby Upland created the concept of a newspaper "written by children for grown folks."

Children's newspaper was instant Burlingame success

Everyone, during summer 1932, wanted to believe that the *Neighborhood News* was a children's endeavor. And, for a few weeks, it was.

A couple of North Burlingame 12-year olds, Billy George and Bobby Upland wanted to start a newspaper, "written by children for grown folks." Before long 70 youngsters were bringing in stories. The weekly filled a need for the Depression-saddled Broadway Development Association. Merchants clamored to advertise.

It seemed that everybody in North Burlingame read the *Neighborhood News*. Circulation reached 1,500.

Although said to be a children's newspaper, weekly production was too demanding for youngsters. Billy's mom did layout. Billy's dad, a lithographer, did the printing. A paid secretary handled hundreds of dollars a week in advertising.

A small building was rented at 1155 California Drive. A press was installed and a union printer hired. Charges were made that child labor laws were being violated. Under threat of a suit by the *Burlingame Advance Star*, publication ceased after two years.

The Lee family and all eight children. Four girls were born before the first son.

LEE FAMILY

LEE FAMILY

Frank Lee and his wife with their four daughters in Colusa on the eve of moving to Burlingame in 1932.

Burlingame's first Chinese family

The first family of Chinese ancestry came to live in Burlingame in 1932. Frank Lee with his wife and eight children—four girls and four boys—encountered major prejudice. Barbers refused to cut the children's hair. Lee found a building lot at 11 Burlingame Avenue, far enough from town that he hoped there would be no objection. A judge unsuccessfully tried to drive the family out.

For years the town's only Asians, the Lees became popular and pioneered desegregation. They opened a cafe on Lorton Avenue. Food was mostly American; the specialty was popovers. Chinese food was served one night a week. Every child worked in the restaurant.

Though unusual, in that he was the only Asian in the school, Bob Lee was elected student body president of Burlingame High in 1947. Frank Lee Jr. became the first Chinese-American Harbor Commissioner in 1969. Bill, later a minister, ran a television repair shop. May (Chan) was employed during World War II as the town's *first* female and *first* Asian postal employee.

TOM GRAY

The Coast Daylight, *considered one of the nation's most beautiful trains, sped daily between San Francisco and Los Angeles.*

BURLINGAME HISTORICAL SOCIETY

Children commuted daily by train to schools beyond Burlingame. These children, about 1925, were boarding a train for Mt. Carmel School in Redwood City.

Trains along the Peninsula

A common Burlingame social event was going to the depot to await the arrival of the *Lark*, the San Francisco-to-Los Angeles streamliner along Southern Pacific's Coast Route. Youngsters especially enjoyed watching clerks in the Post Office car, sorting letters with the speed of a well-oiled machine.

The *Lark*, by the 1940s the nation's premier sleeping car train created for businessmen who made the overnight San Francisco-to-Los Angeles trek, inaugurated coast service in 1910. Train watchers also particularly appreciated the dramatic *Coast Daylight*, which at various times, beginning in 1922, covered the same route. By 1937, the *Daylight*, with matching cars uniquely painted red, orange and black, was considered the "The Most Beautiful Train in the World." Southern Pacific declared that no train on earth had been more photographed.

The *Lark, Daylight, Sunset Limited* (San Francisco to New Orleans beginning in 1901), *Del Monte* (San Francisco-Monterey inaugurated in the 1880s) and other through "name trains" made their single San Mateo County stops in Burlingame for the convenience of residents of the exclusive suburb.

By 1916, more than 40 commute trains (approximately 20 in each direction) stopped daily at Burlingame.

ED ARNOLD

Town resident Ed Arnold on the field at the city park (Washington) May 16, 1931. The Burlingame B's were playing Redwood City.

Burlingame was a baseball town

Baseball was an important part of life in early Burlingame. Sunday mornings were reserved for church, afternoons for baseball.

The town's original baseball organization began in 1911 when the first team played on a field at the corner of Anita Road and Peninsula Avenue. At that game on April 21, a box of cigars was offered to the player who hit the most runs.

Under the auspices of the Burlingame Athletic Association, the team played at County Road and Cypress (after 1912) and at the new Carolan Field (1920). Two years later, called the *Burlingame B's*, it began play at what later was dedicated as Washington Park field.

The Burlingame-San Mateo match-up always drew the largest crowds. Often as many as 3,000 fans were in attendance. Automobiles circled the field creating an outfield fence.

Players, often from other towns, received as much as $5 a game. Fans, who contributed money for team support, elected a board of directors. They appointed a manager. He hired players.

A hat was passed during games to pay for umpires along with balls, bats, uniforms and other equipment.

Other semi-pro baseball teams have played in town. For a time, the local team was the *Burlingame Blues* (a name usually associated with San Mateo's semi-pro team). During the 1940s, the *Burlingame Cardinals* took to the field and in the 1970s, it was the *Burlingame Braves*.

Baseball was a Sunday afternoon pastime in Burlingame.

BURLINGAME PUBLIC LIBRARY

VIRGINIA SAEGER MEITZ

Virginia Saeger posed for photographers as the town's first Miss Burlingame in 1935.

VIRGINIA SAEGER MEITZ

Saeger, among the flowers, was theme girl of the San Mateo County Floral Fiesta in 1936.

Virginia Saeger was first Miss Burlingame

Virginia Saeger graduated from Burlingame High School in 1932. Three years later (1935), Postmaster Joe Gaffey asked her to represent the town at the San Mateo County Floral Fiesta.

Saeger (Meitz) recalled being introduced as the *first* Miss Burlingame from a hastily constructed stage on the green of Bay Meadows Race Track in San Mateo. "That was before any buildings or the exhibition center was built." Burlingame Mayor C.A. Buck made the presentation. Saeger appeared in the latest swimming fashion, a pink fishnet suit built on a foundation of flesh-colored jersey. The revealing apparel was banned from some beaches.

Along with winners from San Bruno, Redwood City, San Mateo and Half Moon Bay, Saeger was awarded a trip to San Diego. "It was all very luxurious," she remembered. At the Burlingame depot, the girls boarded a special sleeping car attached to the Southern Pacific *Owl*.

It was the trip of a lifetime. Elegant accommodations were provided at San Diego's just completed El Cortez Hotel. "They took pictures of us constantly."

Virginia Saeger Meitz, born in 1914, a longtime member and one-time president of the Woman's Club, also was Burlingame's theme girl for the San Mateo County Floral Fiesta in 1936.

Borden's Dairy Delivery Co. absorbed
the Millbrae Dairy. It closed in 1970.

TOM GRAY

Burlingame landmark closes

SAN MATEO HISTORICAL MUSEUM

*The Millbrae Dairy, dating from the 1870s, became one
of the largest milk-producers on the Peninsula.*

The company traced its origin to 1870 when Gold Rush banker-millionaire Darius Ogden Mills started milk production on his Millbrae and Burlingame estate, encompassing several thousand acres, east and west of County Road. By the 1880s, the platform at Millbrae depot was perpetually crammed with milk cans. Trains carted 750 gallons of milk daily to San Francisco, more than a quarter million gallons annually.

Millbrae Dairy continued production until 1938 when it sold to Borden's Dairy Delivery Co. The company's distribution plant, from where milk trucks daily ventured forth, was located at 198 California Drive in Burlingame.

A soda fountain in conjunction with the plant became a town landmark. For years, it was a traditional hangout for the high school crowd and a mecca for socializing.

Borden sales declined steadily throughout Northern California during the 1960s. The Burlingame plant and soda fountain closed in February 1970.

TOM GRAY

Citizens of Burlingame managed to save the Greyhound bus depot from destruction. The landmark became a community meeting place.

Greyhound Depot

The mission revival structure has stood alone in a triangular piece of Burlingame at the corner of Howard Avenue and California Drive since construction in 1939. For half a century it served as the town's Greyhound Bus depot. Town residents came to regard it as one of Burlingame's unique features.

Faced with financial cutbacks and service reduction during the late 1980s, Greyhound asked for release from its $125 a month commitment to the city.

Demolition of the landmark building was an idea abhorrent to many in Burlingame. The town, in 1990, remodeled the structure at a cost of $125,000. More than half the total was donated by Shinnyo-En Buddhism.

The Spanish-style, red-tiled roof remained but a new high-tech stucco finish was applied to the exterior. Thereafter, it was set up as a community meeting area for 15-20 people and used by the city's Park and Recreation Department. At the June 1993 depot reopening, Mayor "Bud" Harrison commented that "although we continue to grow, we're trying to preserve the old-time mysticism of the past."

Theodore Max Lilienthal, chairman of the "Salvage for Victory" drive in San Mateo County, proudly displaying a truckload of tin in front of Peninsula Theatre (April 18, 1942).

Young Johnny Arnold of Burlingame allegedly gave away his toy soldier collection during the "Salvage for Victory" drive during World War II.

Treasure in World War II patriotic scrap

If you listened to Theodore Max Lilienthal in 1942, scrap was the key to American victory in World War II. He appealed to Peninsula residents for tin, rubber, scrap iron, rags and paper to assist in the nation's war effort. Almost 50 percent of every tank, truck, ship and machine gun was made of scrap.

A squad of Burlingame policemen was dispatched to Peninsula Theatre on the Avenue, April 18, 1942, when management staged a "Tin Can Matinee." Twelve hundred kids thronged in; trucks carted away three tons of tin.

Even toys were relegated to the scrap pile. Johnny Arnold of Burlingame proudly took his treasures to the collection point, a service station on El Camino Real. "If you can make five bullets out of an old tin can, you ought to get hundreds out of my extra tough tin soldiers," he declared.

Burlingame sacrificed its proudest possessions. A Spanish-American War cannon was donated. Firemen gave their oldest vehicle, a hand-drawn wagon, and a 300-pound bell once mounted atop Weinberg Hall and rung to summon volunteers.

Federal and local officials gathered to break ground for Burlingame's new post office in 1941.

Post Office

Troops of Boy Scouts and the Burlingame High School Band paraded May 22, 1942, for the dedication of the town's new $225,000 marble-lined post office. Situated south of the Avenue on a huge lot running through from Park Road to Lorton Avenue, the modernistic low building had two entrance ways, one from each street.

A post office had been in existence in Burlingame since 1894 when Ira D. Hoitt, superintendent of a private boy's school in what became Hillsborough, complained of the necessity of going to San Mateo to pick up mail. In June 1894, he was appointed as the first postmaster, although, at the time, there were no quarters available.

George W. Gates, Southern Pacific station manager, was named the second postmaster in 1895. The depot served as the post office. In 1906, it was moved to a drug store on Burlingame Square.

In January 1929, after several additional moves, the post office occupied a plain stucco structure on Primrose Road. In the subsequent 13 years, postal receipts increased 100 percent, necessitating the expanded quarters.

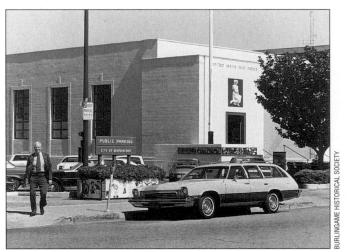

The post office was dedicated in May 1942.

The Broadway Theater on California Drive opened in March 1930.

Broadway-Burlingame

While Broadway began developing as a shopping area in the years after the Armistice in 1918 and it had become a budding shopping area by the 1930s, the post-World War II years were the most important for Broadway-Burlingame. The North Burlingame industrial, commercial and residential area experienced its greatest expansion in history.

During the first five months of 1946, 10 new businesses opened, including the Cover Girl Shop, Kay Burt's Hosiery, Madeline's Apparel and the Broadway Paint Store. Two camera shops opened in April. Thomas J. Callan, owner of a large Colma hog ranch, became an investor along Broadway. In April, his contractors began work on a $70,000 building, one of four major construction projects on the street that year.

"The best for less is always found at Lester's," read the advertisements. In 1946, Lester's sold coffee for 33 cents a pound and a dozen eggs for 49 cents.

At Bergmann's, formerly the Ben Franklin Store, at 1290 Broadway, Easter cards were offered for a nickel. Swim trunks for "dad and lad" sold at the Broadway Toggery for $1–$2.50. Boys' cords were $2.95 a pair. Pure wool socks were $1.

Residential development of Broadway began to grow after the 1906 earthquake.

Commercial establishments along Broadway proliferated following World War I, but the street became a major commercial area in 1946.

Burlingame's business of death

Mortuary architects declared the $200,000 colonial-style building at 2 Park Road a masterpiece when it was completed in June 1946. The structure was the new Crosby-N. Gray & Co. mortuary.

Nebraska-born (1886) William F. Crosby came to Burlingame in 1919. In 1927, he purchased the Wellar Stead undertaking parlor at 23 California Drive.

In 1941, the early San Francisco mortuary company Nathaniel Gray came to town, buying a Park Road funeral parlor run by Frank C. Wyckoff.

Two years later, Crosby and Gray merged. The 1946 building included one chapel which seated 200 and another, arranged like a living room, for 100. The facility had private family rooms adjoining the chapels.

In 1929, William F. Crosby became the chairman of the Burlingame Park Commission. During the 1930s and 1940s, he served as the San Mateo County coroner.

Crosby's son, William J. Crosby, graduated from the University of Southern California and did graduate work at the San Francisco College of Mortuary Science before joining the family business as manager. He served 20 years on the Burlingame City Council and was town mayor on five occasions.

Continuing the family-owned business, John Crosby, a third generation, took over the mortuary operation.

Many of the Peninsula's leading citizens took their last rides in Crosby-N. Gray-owned hearses.

The original chapel at the Park Road mortuary was furnished with wicker chairs rather than pews.

William F. Crosby (center) was one of Burlingame's earliest undertakers. He was succeeded by son William J. and later by grandson John.

A funeral procession at Crosby-N. Gray lined up during the 1950s.

87

Parking problems were increasing along the Avenue in 1956.

BURLINGAME HISTORICAL SOCIETY

BURLINGAME HISTORICAL SOCIETY

Police officer Carl Schwahn increased town revenues after 1946 by citing traffic violators.

Downtown parking mess

More automobiles per capita were owned in the town of Burlingame than any other in the world, or at least so it was reported by journalists in 1922. No precise comparisons were ever offered.

During the early 1930s, longtime zealous Burlingame City Attorney John Davis immersed himself in the problem of parking, dashing off to Oklahoma City to study newfangled devices known as parking meters. There, for a nickel, a meter flashed green light for half an hour. At the end of 30 minutes, a red light flashed, beckoning a cop who came to ticket the car. Test parking meters made their appearance on the streets of Burlingame in 1939.

They became big business in 1946 when the City Council approved the purchase of 771, five-cent-an-hour meters. They cost $79 each. Police Chief R.C. (Jack) Theuer appointed Officer Carl W. Schwahn, who joined the force in 1930, to ride a three-wheeler as the town's first "meter man." His efforts significantly increased town revenues. He retired in 1960.

The house at 1449 Bellevue became headquarters of the Golden Gate Chapter of the American Red Cross.

GOLDEN GATE CHAPTER, AMERICAN RED CROSS

BURLINGAME HISTORICAL SOCIETY

E.J. Sullivan, manager of the Peninsula Theater, and Max Brodie, manager of the San Mateo Theater, making a World War II contribution to Helen Chesebrough of the San Mateo County Chapter of the Red Cross.

Red Cross on Bellevue

Paul A.R. Wessel built the 1449 Bellevue house during the 1920s. On January 24, 1949, after Red Cross members circulated a petition in the neighborhood to secure a variance from the City of Burlingame to allow them to operate in a residential neighborhood, the house was purchased and occupied by the San Mateo County Chapter of the American Red Cross. The acquisition was made possible by a sale to the city of organization property at 260 Primrose Road and by a donation from William B. Kyne of Bay Meadows Race Track.

The house underwent renovation and was dedicated as the *Helen Percy Chesebrough Chapter House*, October 5, 1949. Chesebrough had served with Red Cross in Europe during World War I and returned to become Vice Chairman of the San Mateo County Chapter and Chairman of Volunteers, positions she maintained until her death in 1949.

The San Mateo County Chapter had obtained a charter from the American National Red Cross in 1917. Meetings were initially held at the Burlingame Woman's Club on Park Road.

In 1959, San Francisco Chapter, San Mateo County Chapter and the Sequoia Chapter merged to form the Golden Gate Chapter.

Dedication of the Helen Percy Chesebrough Chapter House of the Red Cross was in 1949. Photographed left to right are Percy Chesebrough, Raymond Barrows, Mrs. Laurance I. Scott, William Hendrickson Taylor and Elizabeth Mack.

Chocolate bunnies, an Easter specialty of Preston's, sold by the thousands during the 1990s.

ARTHUR PRESTON

Proprietor Arthur Preston opened his establishment in 1946.

Preston's Candies

Candy maker Arthur J. Preston, opened his store at 1170 Broadway in October 1946. Then, dozens of independent candy emporiums dotted the Peninsula. A half-century later, Preston's was the only one.

Originally he made all the candy while employing three or four assistants. Each piece was dipped by hand. During the 1940s, two women turned out 150 pounds of candy per day. Preston attributed success to consistency and time-tested recipes that kept old customers coming back.

Easter was his biggest holiday. On the day before Easter of 1992, there were 800 cash register sales. Preston molded between 10,000 and 12,000 Easter eggs per year during the 1990s. Eggs came in chocolate, rocky road and fudge, ranging in weight from two ounces to two pounds.

Preston's was bunny mania for Easter. Bite-sized bunnies, heads on sticks, molded ones on motorcycles, bunnies dressed as cowboys. Some were plain, but others came decorated with eyes, tails and baskets filled with jelly beans.

Preston turned out chocolate cows and fish, even a Golden Gate Bridge. For a golf tournament, he molded hundreds of chocolate golf balls. The Burlingame Country Club once ordered scores of chocolate polo pucks, formed exactly to scale.

Town police cars are lined up near the Park Road City Hall during the 1950s.

Jack Theuer, Chief of Police 1945-1958.

Burlingame Police Department

At the time of incorporation, George E. Jones, Marshal, was the single law enforcement official employed by the town. He retired in 1917 to be replaced by Chief Lewis Cavalier. Upon Cavalier's retirement in 1923, the force had been expanded to five sworn officers.

John J. Harper, a one-time San Francisco policeman and attorney, donned a star as the town's third police chief in December 1923. The following year, with a population of 8,000, in addition to Harper, Burlingame maintained a force of six.

Burlingame was plagued by dust, flies and mosquitoes and inconvenienced by periodic flooding and muddy streets. On the other hand, crime was not a major town concern. During Prohibition, in September 1921, Burlingame police had raided a "full-grown jackass brandy distillery," a common bootlegger's joint almost within the shadow of the Park Road City Hall. The raid jolted residents. The newspaper reported that the town "is pale with shame....Burlingame can no longer stride along with head erect and character undefiled."

Police statistics for 1949 showed there was neither a murder nor robbery that year. Seventy-five burglaries were recorded. Twenty-nine automobiles were stolen, but 25 were recovered. During the same year, Burlingame police recovered 15 additional cars that had been stolen in other cities.

Victor A. Mangini:
Burlingame High School legend

At Burlingame High School,
Vic Mangini became legendary
as a track and football coach.

Vic Mangini was still in Air Force uniform when interviewed for a teaching job in December 1945. The next month he joined the Burlingame High School faculty as assistant football coach and head track coach. In 1958, he shifted to become the assistant principal. He retired in 1980, although his involvement with the high school continued for decades.

Mangini's 12-coaching years, 1946-1958, made him legendary. He helped bring the high school 18 titles. Burlingame won 11 straight victories over San Mateo High School. "The school didn't put pressure on us to win," recalled Mangini. "Any pressure I felt was all my own."

Different times. Teams played in a wooden stadium built by students under the direction of shop teachers. Track hurdles were also made by students. Mangini recalled football games at Palo Alto. "Our players suited up in Burlingame, walked to catch the train and then came back in muddy dirty uniforms. Showers were taken at home."

There were high points in Mangini's coaching. One student became the first in Northern California to break 13 feet in the pole vault, clearing the bar at an amazing 13 feet 2 inches.

Upon retiring from coaching in 1958, Mangini was honored as Burlingame's 19th Citizen of the year. There was a unique parade along El Camino Real and a community banquet at the normally more exclusive Burlingame Country Club.

Burlingame High School student Carol Ann Snarr was official starter of the 1947-1948 Burlingame Invitational Relays. Runners (left to right) are Dan Kaplan, Arlen Gregorio, Mike Darling and Chris Vlassis. Wood stands in the background were made by students under supervision of shop teachers.

Volunteer waitresses in 1947 posed in front of the San Mateo tearoom before its official opening.

50 CENTS

The Burlingame-San Mateo Junior Auxiliary
of the
Stanford Convalescent Home

● **RAFFLE** ●

1st Prize: 1947 NASH AUTOMOBILE
Courtesy of Keough-Hanna Motor Co.
Howard and El Camino, Burlingame

2nd Prize: Case of Scotch Whisky

Date of Drawing: FEBRUARY 1, 1947

No. 854

You need not be present to win

GARDEN CAFE

The Garden Cafe

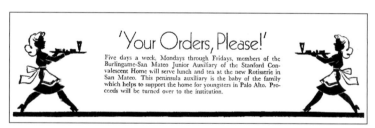

'Your Orders, Please!'

Five days a week, Mondays through Fridays, members of the Burlingame-San Mateo Junior Auxiliary of the Stanford Convalescent Home will serve lunch and tea at the new Rotisserie in San Mateo. This peninsula auxiliary is the baby of the family which helps to support the home for youngsters in Palo Alto. Proceeds will be turned over to the institution.

Its main room was decorated in modern woods with a background of pale yellow walls, a blue canopy ceiling, bird-cage planters and handsome Japanese lanterns. Solid round tables and handsome side buffets were in the redwood-paneled Victorian room. A balcony provided for overflow crowds or special parties. Poodles adorned powder room walls; hunting scenes were in the men's room.

This was the Garden Cafe, which was opened at 1447 Burlingame Avenue in 1953. It was a project of the San Mateo-Burlingame Auxiliary of the Children's Hospital at Stanford. (This later became the Lucile Salter Packard Children's Hospital.) The cafe was operated by the Auxiliary as its commitment to the hospital. Waitresses were volunteers. Salaries and tips were contributed to the hospital.

Auxiliary members began work in the restaurant business in 1947 when they opened a San Mateo tearoom. The move to Burlingame Avenue came in 1953. The Auxiliary also benefitted the hospital through sponsoring tennis and golf tournaments.

An art gallery featuring works of local artists opened in the 1960s. Garden Cafe celebrated 40 years on Burlingame Avenue in 1993.

Streamlined Peninsula Hospital as it appeared when it opened in 1954.

The three-piece switchboard installed in Peninsula Hospital was one of the largest in San Mateo County. It had 20 trunk lines, 82 dial lines and handled 136 phones in hospital rooms.

Peninsula Hospital & Medical Center

After two years of construction, Peninsula Hospital opened its doors on March 1, 1954. Funds for the hospital, $3.9 million, had been raised through bond issues in 1948 and 1952. The sprawling facility, which by the 1990s maintained a staff of 500 physicians and 1,100 nurses and other hospital employees, was constructed on a 23-acre site, along El Camino Real at Trousdale Avenue, on the grounds of the D.O. Mills estate.

Included on the site is the Community Mental Health Center with both inpatient and outpatient facilities and the Peninsula Memorial Blood Bank.

In 1985, Peninsula Hospital merged with Mills Memorial Hospital of San Mateo. Economic realities subsequently forced closure of Mills as an acute care facility. With an expanded role, the Burlingame hospital became known as the Mills-Peninsula Medical Center. By the early 1990s, it provided care for almost 13,000 inpatients annually and emergency service for 24,000 more.

Through additional construction, the hospital has more than doubled in size since 1954.

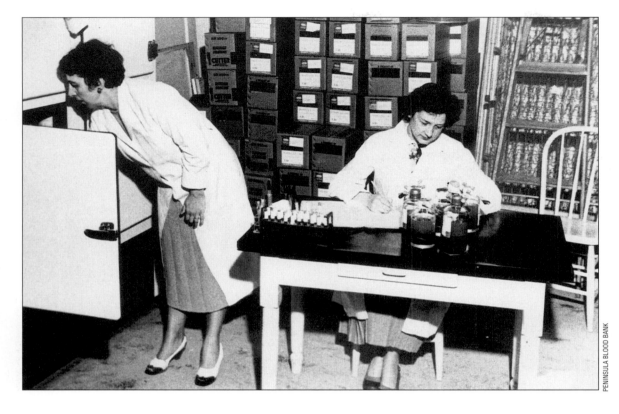

PENINSULA BLOOD BANK

Refrigeration units at the blood bank were initially installed free of charge by the Borden Dairy Delivery Co.

Blood banking on Peninsula

The new building housing the Peninsula Memorial Blood Bank was dedicated near the entrance to Peninsula Hospital in North Burlingame April 25, 1954. The state-of-the-art $210,000 structure was the culmination of a longtime dream.

From its inception in 1942, the San Mateo County Blood Bank, as originally called, had been an innovative and pioneering institution. It was one of the first blood banks in the west. Prior to World War II, a patient whose life depended upon a transfusion often found odds stacked against him. There are four types of blood. Searching for the proper match involved time-consuming testing and tremendous expense.

John Bowler, a pre-war Peninsula donor, remembered being laid on a gurney next to a patient; blood was transferred via a rubber tube.

The blood bank opened on San Mateo Junior College property, near Mills Hospital, May 23, 1942. Its purpose was to service 11 hospitals in San Mateo and Santa Clara counties in addition to supplying blood to military hospitals throughout the Bay Area.

In 1992, after half a century of existence, blood bank officials noted they'd drawn 877,722 units of blood.

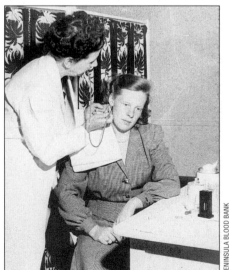

PENINSULA BLOOD BANK

Using oral suction through a rubber tube, a nurse takes a blood sample for typing (1952).

The Chiapelone family was photographed in the nursery about 1950. From left to right are Ann, Laura, John, Charlotte and James. Most of the early plants and trees were cultivated at Home Place, one of the Crocker estates in Hillsborough.

Burlingame Garden Center

James and Laura Chiapelone acquired the little white house, surrounded by the picket fence, at 1427 Chapin in 1942. Four years later Fred Whitman, seeking an outlet for plants he was growing on his mother's (Jenny Crocker Whitman Henderson) Hillsborough estate, suggested that the Chiapelones sell plants in their front yard. Thus was the origin of the Burlingame Garden Center which opened in June 1946.

For the first two years, while her husband was elsewhere employed, the business was run by Laura Chiapelone. "She really knew nothing about running a nursery but she learned fast," remembered her son John, who came to run the business. "She read books and articles, asked questions and really became an expert."

During the Garden Center's early years, it was definitely a family business. As soon as the nursery was on its feet, James gave up his other job and devoted all his effort to the business. "Everybody worked," remarked daughter Ann. "We planted, watered and weeded. John and I were assigned to fill sacks with steer manure that was delivered, in bulk, weekly."

The Garden Center acquired the Farrell house, next door, at 1421 Chapin in 1968. The family rescued it from being razed for a parking lot.

James Chiapelone initially stated that he wanted to sell plants only, not fertilizer, pots, gifts and tools. By the 1990s, such items made up more than 50 percent of Garden Center business.

Burlingame Garden Center as it appeared in 1946 when it opened in the front yard of the Chiapelone home at 1427 Chapin.

The rear view of the Mills home shortly before it was destroyed.

MILLBRAE FIRE DEPARTMENT

Fate of the Mills Estate

The Mills estate constituted a thousand acres of greenbelt extending from Millbrae Avenue to the north border of Ray Park and from El Camino Real into the hills. There were several private lakes and thousands of trees. Although the Mills family preferred to live in New York, this was a Mills fiefdom maintained year around.

In 1946, estate executives requested annexation to Burlingame. But Millbrae, a village originally named for banker and Comstock millionaire D.O. Mills, shouted foul. Millbrae town fathers insisted the estate rightfully belonged to them.

State law seemed explicit. An area to be annexed must physically touch the annexing city. In a rare maneuver, Burlingame annexed a 100-foot wide strip, in all 40 acres, which encircled the estate. This "Chinese Wall," as Burlingame officials called it, created a barrier between the unincorporated estate and Millbrae.

Legal wrangling ensued for almost a decade. Ultimately the estate was divided between the two towns. The Mills house burned in 1954 at the same time Los Angeles developers Paul W. Trousdale and Clint W. Murchinson were beginning to subdivide the property. Bulldozers cleared the land of trees.

MILLBRAE FIRE DEPARTMENT

Happy House *burned to the ground in a dramatic blaze, June 23, 1954.*

Gary Guittard, a fourth generation, as president of the chocolate company in the 1990s, inspects white chocolate drops, manufactured by the millions.

Guittard Chocolate was one of the original industries to be established in Millsdale Industrial Park. At the 1955 groundbreaking were (left to right): James Brett of Coldwell, Banker & Co.; L.E. Weisenberg, manger of Trousdale Development; Charles Rooth, Burlingame's vice-mayor; Horace Guittard, president of the company; Robert Cahill, contractor, and Oscar Person, president of the Burlingame Industrial Association.

Guittard: the house that chocolate built

Guittard Chocolate Company traced its origin to 1868 when French immigrant Étienne Guittard began making chocolate in San Francisco.

In 1955, the company moved to the Millsdale Industrial Park, laid out by developer Paul Trousdale, off of Rollins Road in Burlingame. This was one of the first industries to build on one-time pasture land owned by D.O. Mills. The land cost Guittard $50 an acre.

During the 1880s, the firm sold its product under 14 different labels. Advertising noted that chocolate was recommended by physicians "to persons of delicate constitution as a strengthener" and as a preventative against a litany of unpleasant ailments, including heart disease.

By the 1990s, the company was the principal supplier of chocolate to Baskin-Robbins ice cream makers. Ninety-five percent of all chocolate used by See's Candies, an average of eight million pounds a year, was also supplied by Guittard. It was delivered in liquid form by a fleet of stainless steel, glass-lined tanker trucks, each containing 50,000 pounds of chocolate.

For close to half a century, the aroma of Guittard's has permeated the atmosphere of Burlingame.

Firefighters in front of the California Drive station during a flood of the 1950s. The photo has become legendary.

BURLINGAME HISTORICAL SOCIETY

Flooding in Burlingame

Over a century, Burlingame spent millions of dollars controlling surging flood waters that periodically plagued the town. During the 1950s, city engineers transformed a number of streams into pipelines to carry off water. Two 90-inch pipes were run under Oak Grove Avenue from California Drive to the bay. Still identifiable, thereafter, were Burlingame, Ralston, Terrace, Sanchez, Easton and Mills creeks.

Following flooding of the 1950s, gates were installed at the mouth of El Portal Creek, forming the boundary with Millbrae, seen on the land surface only from the railroad tracks to the Bay. Closed at high tide (in conjunction with heavy rain), the gates prevented dangerous inundation of the town by Bay waters.

As late as the 1920s, during rains, Burlingame youngsters sailed boats along California Drive. Water frequently swirled through businesses and invaded the train depot. The Broadway Theater on California Drive was often closed during the 1930s and 1940s when the orchestra pit and the first rows of seats flooded.

The 1950s photograph of Burlingame firefighters in front of the California Drive firehouse has become legendary. When that station was rebuilt in the 1990s, its foundation was raised a foot in the effort to deny later access to surging water.

BURLINGAME HISTORICAL SOCIETY

Until the 1950s when the town began spending millions of dollars on flood control, overflowing creeks and high tides caused frequent flooding.

Peninsula Theatre, considered the ultimate in luxury, opened in 1926.

The Peninsula Theatre, known for its ornate facade, became the Fox Burlingame in 1957.

A movie palace on the Avenue

The Garden continued as the town's sole movie house until the $500,000 Peninsula Theatre premiered October 12, 1926.

On the Avenue's south side and farther west than the Garden, this magnificent Spanish medieval-style playhouse, was the most luxurious entertainment palace south of San Francisco. Investors spared no expense. It had the largest stage between San Francisco and San Jose and a 1,033-pipe Robert Morton organ capable of imitating sounds of a 200-piece orchestra.

Much civic pride was exhibited in the electric sign containing 3,500 blinking bulbs which could be seen for miles. General admission was 40 cents; loges went for 60 cents. Seating capacity was almost 2,000.

The Peninsula closed for installation of sound equipment in 1927 when "talkies" first appeared. It was renamed the Fox Burlingame in 1957 and closed in 1975. When town trustees feared the downtown theater would be taken over by operators of hardcore pornography, they ordered it locked. The structure later was transformed into a shopping mall.

Burlingame High School String Orchestra

The Burlingame High School String Orchestra, created in 1952 by teacher-director Lawrence Short, was accustomed to accolades. In 1956, 1957 and 1958, it won the highest ratings at the Northern California Music Festival competitions. In 1958, the 29 girls and 5 boys were asked to play for the National Convention of Music Educators in Los Angeles.

Then came the ultimate invitation, to attend the Brussels World's Fair in August 1958. The State Department request did not come with expense money. Students were expected to raise $40,000.

What followed was one of the great fund-raising efforts in Burlingame history. Most people agreed with Short that "a performance by a public school orchestra would do more than any professional group to symbolize American culture to Europeans."

Checks poured in from service organizations, businesses and labor unions. Collection containers were placed in stores throughout the county. Students solicited funds door-to-door. San Mateo, Hillsdale and Capuchino high schools staged concerts and played at every railroad station along the Peninsula.

The tour was an amazing triumph. Students won international acclaim, playing in Copenhagen for the Third Annual International Music Educators Convention. Later, they played for 7,000 at the American Pavilion at the World's Fair. In all, students visited eight European countries in 27 days and played six concerts.

Burlingame's String Orchestra played special concerts to raise money for their trip to Copenhagen and Brussels.

Students flew Pan American World Airways on a polar route to Europe.

Burlingame High School String Orchestra members sharing refreshment at the American Pavilion in Brussels.

Church diversity

Town visitors are often struck by Burlingame's church diversity. Conspicuous along El Camino Real are the onion domes of the Russian Orthodox Church of All Saints, completed in 1964. With a hint of eastern mystery, the building is the summer residence of the Metropolitan, head of the Russian Church in exile.

Occupying one-time Hoover School is the headquarters of Shinnyo-En Buddhism, fastest-growing Buddhist sect in Japan. During the 1960s, the sect began expanding outside Japan. Its goal was to make Buddhist teaching more understandable.

The old Burlingame school was redecorated as a temple and teaching facility where more than a hundred studied to become Buddhist priests.

While Seventh Day Adventists commenced worship in homes of members in 1906, their Spanish-style church near Hillsborough Town Hall on El Camino Real was completed in 1936. Well-known for three century-old, cast bronze bells, the church fell victim to arson and was gutted in 1990. The new exterior followed 1930s styling. It reopened in 1994.

The Broadway (Encore) Theater at 1157 California Drive, closed for years, reopened in 1989, housing the American Gnostic Church. The religion predates Christianity and is derived from the Greek word for knowledge.

Broadway Theater became the Encore. Closed during the 1970s, it opened a decade later as the American Gnostic Church.

The Rev. Stefan Pavlenko standing in front of the Russian Orthodox Church of All Saints, 1986.

Charlie Brown in Burlingame

Lee Mendleson Productions became a Burlingame force in 1963 when it produced its first television network special, *A Man Named Mays*, a documentary in which cameramen followed baseball great Willie Mays throughout an entire season. Critics called it "a television home run."

Since, Lee Mendleson Productions has produced more than 300 television shows for each of the major networks. In the process, the company won a dozen Emmys and a handful of Peabody Awards.

The company created all the popular Peanuts specials including the prize-winning *Charlie Brown's Christmas* that first aired in 1965. *Cathy* and *Garfield*, also recognized as among the best, are animated features also produced by Mendleson.

Top Hollywood personalities have participated in live-action shows. These have included Paul Newman, Joanne Woodward, David Niven, Henry Fonda, Bing Crosby and Gene Kelly.

Writing and planning were done in Burlingame; animation and much of the actual production were done in Hollywood.

For years, Lee Mendleson Productions was a Burlingame landmark. The business occupied a structure on Chapin Avenue opposite the Garden Center. The face of the building was decorated with characters which figured largely in Mendleson's programming.

*The water landing of the
Japan Air Lines jet was
accomplished without
injury. Passengers were in
almost jovial spirits when
rafts were towed ashore.*

Japan Air Lines DC-8
lands short of runway

Friday morning, November 22, 1968, Japan Air Lines Flight 2 from
Tokyo to New York, with 96 passengers and 11 crewmen aboard, went down
in the swirling waters of the Bay off Burlingame.

Shiga, a giant DC-8, crashed while making an approach to San
Francisco International Airport, approximately three miles short of the
runway. Hospitals were alerted and ambulances summoned.

Fearing the worst, at Burlingame's Peninsula Hospital, the disaster
plan was activated. Almost 100 doctors were in the building at the time.
Along with nurses and support personnel, they rushed to disaster positions.
Wheelchairs and stretchers were moved to the hospital's emergency
entrance.

Switchboard operators alerted more doctors. Within an hour, scores were
en route to the hospital. Police established roadblocks to facilitate movement of casualties.

The crash was a million to one shot. The DC-8, with its landing gear down, had come to rest
on solid Coyote Point Reef in the "Bay of Burlingame." Another few yards, it would have sunk
like a rock. *Shiga* was the most successful ditching of a jet airliner in history. The touchdown was
"smooth" and seemed "routine." No one was even slightly injured.

*Burlingame emergency plans
were put into play in 1967
when a Japan Air Lines plane
belly flopped into the Bay.*

Burlingame residents contributed money to pay for an ambulance, delivered to Cuernavaca in 1969.

Sister City

President Dwight D. Eisenhower established a *People-to-People Program* in 1956 to promote international friendship through contacts between people of different countries.

A Burlingame Sister City committee was created and, in 1964, recommended establishment of a unique relationship between Burlingame and Cuernavaca in Mexico.

Presidente Municiple Valentin Lopez Gonzalez, mayor of Cuernavaca, and a dozen city officials visited Burlingame in 1964. Subsequently, a park in North Burlingame was named Cuernavaca in honor of Burlingame's sister city.

In January 1969, after months of agonizing red tape involving both the American and Mexican governments, Burlingame's Ben Hechinger, president of the Sister City Association, began a 2,700-mile, six-day drive to deliver an industrial ambulance to the people of Cuernavaca. The ambulance, a gift from the people of Burlingame, was loaded with therapeutic equipment and toys for the children of the Mexican town.

Members of Burlingame's Sister City Committee visited Cuernavaca, Mexico, in 1964. An El Camino Real bell was one of many gifts presented to the people of the Mexican city. The priest in this picture is flanked by Burlingame Councilman William J. Crosby (left) and Valentin Lopez Gonzalez, mayor of Cuernavaca.

Experts described the 1970 City Hall as "Burlingame architecture."

Crowds gathered for City Hall dedication ceremonies April 4, 1970.

Burlingame City Hall

In 1945, the ivy-covered 1914 City Hall at 267 Park Road was declared to be inadequate for a town growing as rapidly as Burlingame.

A new city hall, designed by the architectural firm of Kahl, Howell and Whifler, with 27,000 square feet, was built and dedicated April 4, 1970. Located at the intersection of Primrose Road and Bellevue Avenue, the new two-story government center, was three times larger than the old. It housed the town's administrative offices and included sub-level parking.

Architects adopted a circular floor plan which they aptly described as "Burlingame architecture."

The old Park Road City Hall symbolized the town's relaxed past. The new building, constructed around circular city council chambers allegedly symbolized its future. A lighted fountain splashed water outside the council chambers. The new municipal administration building was constructed at a cost of $840,512.

Art in the Park

Street and outdoor fairs have long been a Burlingame tradition. Some of the earliest, dating from 1908, when the streets were festooned with colored Japanese lanterns, were sponsored by the Woman's Club, specifically to raise money for civic beautification.

In 1970, Carter Church, a student at Burlingame High School, came up with the idea for *Art in the Park*, an open-air art show in Washington Park next to the high school where people could surround themselves with arts and crafts.

What became an annual event steadily increased in popularity. By its twenty-fifth anniversary, 20,000 members of the community participated.

In 1995, *Art in the Park* featured jazz and dance groups along with Magic Pearl Puppets for youngsters. Reflecting an increased fear in crime, the police department provided free fingerprinting for children. An increasingly health conscious public sought out the fire department booth where young firefighters checked blood pressure.

Nonprofit organizations set up specialty food and information booths. Participants included every Burlingame service club, the Historical Society, the Chamber of Commerce and Burlingame High School.

This poster was used to advertise the 25th anniversary of Art in the Park (1995).

The General Frank M. Coxe
*was a familiar sight on San
Francisco Bay as a tour boat.*

A *town of restaurants*

During the decades after 1960, increasing numbers of restaurants came to dominate Burlingame's downtown. Ultimately, the City Council placed restrictions on the numbers which would be allowed. Forty was the maximum number in the area of Burlingame Avenue and 23 were permitted along Broadway.

Those seeking food diversity or ambience had no difficulty finding it. One of the town's most unusual restaurant ventures was the *General Frank M. Coxe*, a one-time San Francisco excursion boat which was towed to the Burlingame marsh in 1971. Thereafter, the boat which had carried thousands of excursionists on the Bay was reborn as the *Pattaya Princess* or, more commonly, *The Showboat*. The small craft emerged from renovation complete with an ersatz side-wheel. The restaurant served seafood and continental cuisine. It closed after a decade. The deserted boat began settling into the marsh, becoming a decaying, tilting landmark.

*Restaurant-goers found the old
tour boat transformed into*
The Showboat, *perched on
the Burlingame marsh in 1971.*

Peninsula Tennis Club

The Peninsula Tennis Club was built on what had once been a portion of the Corbitt horse ranch. In 1934, the property was purchased by tennis enthusiasts who, having decided the year before to create a private club, formed the Peninsula Tennis Club. On the eastern edge of Burlingame High School, the property was acquired for $4,500. To offset expenses, members agreed to pay 25 cents per month for two years. Dedication was July 21, 1935; a clubhouse was completed in 1937.

Between 1949 and 1989, this was the site of the prestigious National Hardcourt Championships for boys and girls. A number of leading players demonstrated skill on club courts. These included Jimmy Connors and Billie Jean Moffit King (1970). Other luminaries who appeared were Roscoe Tanner (1968), Eliot Teltscher (1976), Brian Teacher (1972), Brian Gottfried (1969), Dick Stockton (1969) and Pam Shriver (1977).

Hometown favorites were San Mateo's Ann Kiyomura, who won eight national championships and a women's doubles championship at prestigious Wimbledon (1975). Erik van Dillen, raised in San Mateo Park, won three junior championships at the Peninsula Tennis Club. He was ranked No. 1 in the United States in men's doubles (1971-1973). Van Dillen played doubles at Wimbledon and was on the U.S. Davis Cup team (1969-1976).

Since 1952, the Peninsula Tennis Club has also hosted the California State Seniors Tournament.

Billie Jean Moffit (King)

Erik van Dillen

Ann Kiyomura

Jimmy Connors

Throughout the town's history, residents have shown a determination to maintain quality education. Just one of a thousand dedicated teachers, Harriet Henderson is pictured with her fourth graders at Pershing School during the 1925-1926 school year.

BURLINGAME HISTORICAL SOCIETY

Burlingame Community for Education

Between 1970 and 1983, Burlingame schools lost 44 percent of their enrollment, going from 2,750 students to 1,209.

Declining enrollments accompanied by state budgetary cutbacks during the 1970s prompted creation of the Burlingame Community for Education. It was a move by parents to overcome the shortfall. The all-volunteer, nonprofit corporation received official tax-exempt status in 1980.

The foundation was a joint effort by the school district, the community and the Chamber of Commerce. Leaders saw it as an opportunity for town residents to "invest in education." Money raised was used to restore enrichment programs, upgrade school libraries and media centers, and provide self-improvement grants for teachers.

In its first generation of existence, the Burlingame Community for Education raised $610,000. Foundation president Carol Tanzi commented in 1997: "Build the foundation of education for the young and they will go on to build the house of knowledge throughout their lives."

NORMAN KAVANAUGH

Newspaper readers learned that Burlingame firefighters had donated their historic bell to the World War II scrap drive.

Historic relics saved

Burlingame's fire department donated generously to the World War II "Salvage for Victory" campaign. The department's first piece of apparatus, a delicate, hand-drawn chemical wagon, was donated for scrap. Also scrapped was a bell, installed atop Weinberg Hall in 1910, to summon volunteer firemen. So said newspapers.

The historic bell had in fact been packed away during the 1920s after Weinberg Hall, upon which it had been mounted, was torn down.

Rediscovered during the "Salvage" campaign, the bell rang again as a symbol of sacrifice. Thereafter, it was quietly sent to the U.S. Merchant Marine School at Coyote Point (1943). At war's end, the bell was returned to Burlingame and again hidden away for two decades.

Later, it was mounted in front of the Fire Department headquarters on Rollins Road. Following reconstruction of the station on California Drive, the original bell was placed there.

Inexplicably, the cherished chemical wagon was also spared the scrap heap. Throughout the 1980s and 1990s, a proud possession of the Burlingame Fire Department, it was regularly displayed at town celebrations.

BURLINGAME FIRE DEPARTMENT

Burlingame's fire chief announced in 1943 that Chemical No. 1, the town's original apparatus had been put to the torch in the name of World War II victory.

*Installed above Broadway
in 1927, the sign became a
symbol of the North
Burlingame shopping area.*

*When threatened with
demolition during the 1980s,
the Broadway arch became the
object of local nostalgia.*

A *sign became
a point of civic pride*

The arching electric sign was erected in 1922 at
El Camino Real and Howard Avenue. Its message:
"To Pacific City."

But Pacific City, the amusement park, folded in
1923. Three years later the darkened sign was sold to
the Broadway Development Association. They
acquired it in lieu of a $500 outstanding debt.

Reworded with 14-inch porcelain letters spelling
out "Broadway-Burlingame," it was moved and
installed above Broadway at California Drive,
indicating the entrance to the shopping district. Sign
dedication was April 23, 1927.

Thereafter the sign, a symbol of Broadway-
Burlingame, experienced 60 years of neglect. A surge
of local nostalgia in 1987 resulted in an effort to save
the sign from decay and possible demolition.

A "Save the Arch" campaign generated public
support. Citizens contributed to the effort. The
Broadway Merchants Association sponsored an essay
contest: "What the Broadway Arch Means to Me."

The sign was removed, reconstructed and
reinstalled. In the process it was repositioned 50 feet
west of its original location. The cost of the process
was $50,000. Rededication of the Broadway-
Burlingame arch was November 26, 1988.

SCOTT BUSCHMAN

Hyatt Regency SFO

Much excitement was generated along the Peninsula in 1959 when the Hyatt House, a 303-room "fly-in hotel" was opened on filled marshland east of Bayshore near Broadway-Burlingame. But the gala paled by comparison to the one that accompanied the opening of the company's new $117 million 793-room hotel in July 1988.

No Peninsula building could compare. It had the largest convention facility in San Mateo County. Visitors found an atrium filled with a forest of 60-foot bamboo, ficus trees and 1,500 green and flowering plants. There was a cascading waterfall, along with streams and pools.

Barely a year old when the Loma Prieta earthquake shattered the Peninsula, the Hyatt Regency SFO suffered grievous damage. Repairs required closure for 10 months. Engineers discovered major structural damage and deep cracks two stories high in some of the inside load-bearing walls. Repair cost $12 million. With lost bookings, the overall loss to Hyatt was approximately $24 million.

Because of its close proximity to the airport, filled land east of Bayshore Freeway became an unexpected bonanza for the town. The Sheraton Hotel (later the Park Plaza) opened 1974; Crown Plaza San Francisco International Airport greeted guests in 1983; San Francisco Airport Marriott was completed in 1985; Doubletree Hotel and Embassy Suites rolled out their welcome mats in 1986.

By 1997, Burlingame boasted 3,340 hotel rooms. The projected hotel tax income for 1997-1998 was $10.6 million. Hotels, restaurants and related facilities east of the freeway accounted for 52 percent of the city's income.

The luxurious Hyatt Regency SFO, located on the east side of Bayshore near Broadway, was heavily damaged during the earthquake of 1989 and closed for almost a year.

WHITTAKER PHOTOGRAPHY

*Proud firemen displayed their
equipment on the opening day
of the new California Drive
fire station in December 1929.*

Firehouse, 1997

Restoration of the fire station

Town trustees were disappointed in 1990 when informed that the town's most elegant firehouse, at 799 California Drive, failed to meet earthquake standards. That station, costing $38,200, had been completed in 1929 and dedicated November 11, 1930.

Should doors shift or the facade tilt, vehicles would be trapped inside. Furthermore, the original doors had been made for smaller vehicles than the department then used. Modern trucks had only a few inches of clearance.

Rather than destroy the 60-year old relic, the city opted to build a new $3 million station on the same site. Appearing the same as the old, the new one was to have 20 percent more space.

A unique design called for a styrofoam-like substance to cover a steel frame. The new roof was ornamented with four-foot decorative urns. But unlike the original concrete urns, declared hazardous and removed during the 1960s, reproductions were fashioned from fiberglass. Roof tiles from the old structure were utilized on the new.

The 1929 station was designed by the *firm* of Willis Polk & Company. Architectural historians didn't object to the structural alteration because Polk himself had not designed the building.

The California Drive firehouse remained the town's only one until 1950 when Station No. 2 at 2832 Hillside Drive opened. Station No. 3, at 1399 Rollins Road, the departmental headquarters, went into service in 1962.

Presidential visit cost Burlingame plenty

President George Bush with an entourage of aides, secretaries and security guards flew into San Francisco International Airport, October 28, 1990. The purpose was a fundraising breakfast the following morning at William Boyd's Hillsborough home.

Bush stayed overnight at the Hyatt Regency SFO. Nine local jurisdictions including the California Highway Patrol put personnel under the direction of the United States Secret Service. There was a total of 101 police officers on station at the Hyatt. The greatest agency cost, $10,000, was borne by Burlingame. The town provided 46 people for 304 hours of work.

Burlingame City Council members rankled about whether or not to charge the Republican Party. Police Chief Alfred Palmer stated: "As much as I think highly of the office, I can't afford to have the President come every week."

Hyatt management wasn't dismayed. The President's visit booked the equivalent of 650 rooms during preparations and the actual stay.

ALFRED PALMER

Burlingame Police Chief Alfred Palmer greeted President George Bush at the Hyatt Regency SFO in 1990. The chief was miffed at the cost of the presidential visit.

*Burlingame Police
Department's supervan was
a creation of Chief Alfred
Palmer in response to the
Loma Prieta earthquake.*

TOM GRAY

MIKE SPINELLI PHOTOGRAPHY

*Alfred (Fred) Palmer, Chief of
Police, reflected relaxed dress codes
of the late 20th century by seldom
wearing a uniform.*

Police Department's supervan

The donations of 100 businesses and service organizations in 1993, helped transform a one-time $4,000 bread and bakery truck into a $75,000 state-of-the-art Burlingame Police Department emergency service vehicle. The 14-foot, 1985 GMC van was the largest police-owned vehicle in the county.

Designed to serve in major emergencies as a mobile communications center and command post, this vehicle was equipped with police, fire and public works radios in addition to cellular telephones, computers, video fax machines and a cable television line.

The van was the idea of Police Chief Alfred Palmer in response to communications difficulties encountered during the Loma Prieta earthquake of 1989. It gave Burlingame police the ability to communicate with any police or fire agency in the state.

Its use was not restricted simply to Burlingame; but was to be loaned to whatever Peninsula law enforcement agency needed it.

Historic swearing in

The Burlingame City Council meeting, June 2, 1997, was one of the most unique in the history of the town. Both a new police chief and a fire chief were sworn in. Gary Missel, a police commander and 24-year member of the Burlingame force, took over from Chief Alfred Palmer.

William Reilly, a fire department veteran who joined the force in 1972, was sworn in as the new departmental head to replace retiring Chief Malcolm Towns.

This was the first time that both chiefs had been sworn in simultaneously. The promotions became effective June 9, 1997.

History was made at the Burlingame City Council meeting June 2, 1997, when a new police chief and fire chief were sworn in simultaneously. Gary Missel (left) became police chief and William Reilly was sworn in as fire chief.

MIKE SPINELLI PHOTOGRAPHY

Beginning as early as 1915, because of its trees, the piece of State Highway between Millbrae and San Mateo became the most recognizable in California.

Trees along El Camino Real

The Peninsula's Bay shore was a windswept, uninteresting stretch of marsh and prairie in the late 1870s when Scottish landscape gardener John McLaren was retained by landowners to plant trees along the dirt trail known as County Road.

From San Mateo to the Mills estate, elm trees were interspersed with fast-growing Australian gum (eucalyptus) which were to be removed within a few years. Meanwhile, they provided wind protection for the delicate elms. But the gums took over; the elms failed to prosper.

Residents came to treasure the tree-lined boulevard. In 1913, when a proposal was made to cut trees, the mayor promised that anyone caught doing so would be jailed.

In 1916, for safety reasons, hundreds of people demanded tree removal. Pleas fell on deaf ears. When an effort was made in 1934 to cut 19 giants, the Woman's Club linked arms with the Chamber of Commerce to prevent it.

Workers resurfacing El Camino Real in the 1990s declared that 115 trees required removal. The suggestion generated outrage. The California Department of Transportation received letters from all over the state on behalf of the eucalyptus umbrella that had come to represent Burlingame. Support for the trees was almost unanimous. Highway engineers re-evaluated their problems; ultimately only 19 trees were removed.

Afterword

The evolution of a village or community is a perfectly respectable and rewarding subject for social historians. As a matter of fact, though some might disagree, local history is really the story of the United States.

Frequently retold tales of national politicians and presidential personalities, taxes and treaties along with wars and depressions—traditional topics of the most learned historians—tell a reader almost nothing about what life was all about for typical hardworking Americans. Yet, discovering the day-to-day existence of the people is often an impossible endeavor. Even professional historians encounter ongoing frustrations. In the search for Burlingame, a suburb of a major American city and distinguished by many notable citizens, there was no road map to follow.

With one small exception, no books have previously been done on the town's history. In 1977, the Burlingame Historical Society published a brief booklet, *Burlingame: lively memories— a pictorial review* edited by Barbara Evans. This excellent work, which quickly became a collector's item, contained a number of first-person accounts of early Burlingame.

Otherwise, in preparing the present book, the authors were required to rely on newspaper accounts, city documents and personal interviews with longtime residents of the town.

The authors asked some questions for which answers were never satisfactorily found. According to Jack Theuer, an early police chief, George E. Jones, who headed the department during the town's first years, held the title "Marshal," not "Chief." And whereas this appears to have been true, it is obvious from the documents that Jones considered himself Burlingame's first Chief of Police. His photograph in uniform indicates clearly that the medallion on his hat states "Chief." Philip W. Alexander and Charles P. Hamm who wrote the *History of San Mateo County* (1916) state emphatically that he was "Chief of Police." It would appear that he was both "Marshal" and "Chief of Police." That is to say, back then, the two titles seem to have been used interchangeably.

But readers are often unforgiving about even the smallest mistake in local history. "That's not the way I remember it," is a frequent lament. "These aren't local people," was a comment tossed at writers who once referred to the interurban electric trolley which ran along the Peninsula until 1949 as "Car 40." "Correction," said Burlingame critics. "It was the 40 Line, the 40 Car but *never* Car 40." That is, except for other Burlingame old-timers who adamantly insisted it was in fact "Car 40" and never anything else.

Traditionally it is believed that there was no Burlingame school before 1912. In fact, *Burlingame School* was built in early 1906.

Documents can lie. According to official papers, Burlingame's first fire bell, a gift to the town by the Woman's Club in 1910, was scrapped as part of a "Salvage for Victory" campaign during World War II. But, in the 1990s, that identical bell was put on permanent display in front of the California Drive firehouse. Odd.

There are dozens of similar conflicts. Many mysteries remain. Authors did determine this. In Burlingame, as in other towns and cities across America, what is true *is* often not nearly as important as what people *believe* to be true.

In attempting to ferret out the truth of Burlingame's past, the authors are particularly grateful for the historical archive and collection of the Burlingame Historical Society. This small but vibrant organization was established during the Bicentennial of the nation in the 1970s.

Were it not for the efforts of its members in meticulously finding, collecting and cataloging documents and photographs, a book like *Burlingame: City of Trees* would not have been possible. Special thanks are due to Marilyn Short, archivist of the Burlingame Historical Society, who gave generously of her time, taking part in a historical treasure hunt of six months duration.

Because of a lack of published books on the subject, authors delved into the early editions of the *Burlingame Advance*, the *Burlingame Star* and the *Burlingame Advance Star*, the North Burlingame *Neighborhood News* and the *Burlingame-Hillsborough Boutique & Villager*. Burlingame did not exist in a vacuum. Many stories of local interest were also found in the *San Mateo Times*, the *San Mateo News Leader* and virtually all of the major San Francisco newspapers.

These newspapers proved to be important primary sources. Their news sections were valuable. But the feature stories, sports and society columns and even advertisements offered insights into the character of the town and its residents that could be found nowhere else.

There will be those who scoff, saying "never believe what you read in a newspaper." And it is true, written in haste, newspapers often make errors. Throughout the years, however, the

best ongoing documentation of day-to-day life in the nation and its towns has been provided by journalists. They have succeeded where scholars have failed.

Thanks to newspapers, we discovered changing prices of food and clothing. We identified a population determined to make its town a comfortable place to live. We found young boys happily sailing their boats along flooded California Drive and identified hazardous driving conditions along County Road. We found a profile of a town which valued a good library, good education and churches of all variety.

Assembling this book became a community project. Burlingame city officials opened their storage rooms and dusted off their oldest files. City Manager Dennis Argyres, city engineers, city planners, the police, fire and school departments all contributed. City Clerk Judith Malfatti deserves special thanks.

Historical contributions came from restaurants, fraternal and service organizations, even the Peninsula Blood Bank. Alfred Escoffier, Burlingame City Librarian, and his reference staff dipped into the darkest recesses of the institution, managing to uncover a few great treasures—remembering all the while that a priceless local historical treasure might be defined as a single unseen photo or a descriptive letter shedding light on another era.

Town residents provided both stories and photographs. Tom Gray, who has been in and out of Burlingame for more than half a century, made his vast collection of photographs available to us. The San Mateo County Historical Association also provided assistance.

No project could have been packed with so much pleasure. Thanks to the efforts of so many, in *City of Trees* we are able to offer a unique and often charming slice of Americana.

Michael Svanevik & Shirley Burgett
Summer 1997

Burlingame's Main Library

Almost 300 gathered for "An Elegant Affair," September 27, 1997, for a sneak preview of Burlingame's new Main Library. The gala preceding the October 4 grand opening was sponsored by Burlingame Library Foundation.

In 1994, after seismic studies indicated that there were inadequacies in the old library structure, Burlingame's City Council authorized plans for a new building. A unique plan incorporated the existing Children's and References rooms, designed by architect Ernest L. Norberg in 1930 and the Roger and Jean Hunt Duncan property adjacent to the building. The result was a newly expanded and unified library.

While the new library was made possible primarily by city funds, generous donations by Joan and Ralph Lane, Roger and Jean Duncan and other socially conscious town citizens brought about this genuinely unique hall of learning.

The remodeled Burlingame Main Library as it neared completion in summer 1997. The characteristic facade of the old building was incorporated into the new.

BURLINGAME PUBLIC LIBRARY

During the summer of 1997, a worker is seen replacing the library's original tile shingles.

Reconstruction of the Main Library in 1997 maintained a building with early Burlingame characteristics but transformed it into a center for 21st-century learning.

Past meets present and future

In creating the new Main Library, there was obvious reverence for the past. Many details of the 1930 library were preserved or duplicated. Original wood ceiling trusses marked the interior; the 17th-century romantic tapestry, a gift to the library which had hung in the entry for decades, was rehung for the enjoyment of patrons. "Open Book" pilasters on exterior walls were retained.

Under the direction of City Librarian Alfred H. Escoffier, planners, recognizing the importance of access to electronic information, were not bound by the past but focused on the present and the future. The result was a center for 21st century learning. Fifty computer terminals were installed for use in addition to study areas where patrons could plug in laptop computers.

The library's on-line public catalog listed the collection at over 200,000 books and magazines. Patrons were assured unrestricted access to the Internet and other electronic information sources.

Traditional support of the library was augmented by book sales and programs sponsored by the all-volunteer Friends of the Library. The Burlingame Library Foundation, a nonprofit organization established in 1995 by community leaders, was created to "solicit financial support for a growing place of learning" and to supplement services, not possible with city funding.

While in 1929 architect Ernest L. Norberg designed the romantic Tuscan library on Primrose to be built for $65,000, the 1997 building (on the same site) was $9.6 million. Costs with shelving, furnishings, equipment and collateral expenses came to $13 million.

School libraries, one of the victims of budget cuts, received annual support from the Burlingame Community for Education.

Music programs, lost in the budget cutting frenzy, were revived by funds provided by BCE.

Burlingame Community for Education

Necessity is the precursor of invention.

Political, social and economic forces in the 1970s and early 1980s resulted in bad news for California's public schools. Frustrated by steadily escalating taxes, voters "revolted" by passing Proposition 13, a ballot measure which capped property tax rates—a major source of school funding—and required voter approval of virtually all future tax increase proposals.

Public schools were a principal casualty of the tax revolt. Schools now competed with other vital public services, such as police and fire agencies, for their share of a shrinking pie. California's public school system, long-envied by much of the U.S., became a tax-cut orphan. Spending per child plummeted.

To preserve funding for teacher salaries and the basic curriculum, budgets for many other programs—including music, after school enrichment and technology—were reduced or eliminated in many school districts. For Burlingame, a community that had long enjoyed a reputation for stellar public schools, it was a terribly frustrating time.

BCE funding helped create technology labs, allowing students to build computer skills.

Finding a solution: BCE

Within Burlingame, frustration resulting from the tax cuts bred invention.

Why not create a private, nonprofit foundation to raise money for Burlingame schools? A partnership was formed bringing together the schools, the parents and the Burlingame Chamber of Commerce. From clear necessity and sheer determination the Burlingame Community for Education Foundation (BCE) was born.

Since its founding in 1980, the Burlingame Community for Education became a well-recognized, vital source of financial support for the school district's five elementary campuses. Roosevelt School re-opened in fall 1997, becoming the district's fifth primary school site. Burlingame Intermediate was the single middle school.

The BCE's fundraising activities traditionally included a fall direct-mail campaign to target all Burlingame families, and a spring dinner dance with strong support from the Chamber of Commerce and many local businesses.

Between 1992 and 1996, BCE raised and contributed over $450,000 to Burlingame school. Funds were used for computer labs, music instruction, libraries and teacher grants for innovative classroom use.

Burlingame took great pride in its high-quality public school. The community's visionary leadership led to the creation of BCE. Thousands of Burlingame school students, families and business owners have reaped the benefits of that pride and vision.

The Burlingame Community for Education Foundation was built on contributions from families and Burlingame businesses.

INDEX